The Response to Intervention Handbook

Thank you for all you do!

Andrea Ogonosky
12/3/18

The Response to Intervention Handbook

SECOND EDITION

Reenergizing Elementary RtI Systems of Support

ANDREA OGONOSKY

ED311

Austin, Texas

First Printing: April 2018
Second Printing: August 2018

ISBN 978-1-947753-02-0

To Dr. Gail Cheramie, my friend and mentor.
I know I would not be the person and professional that I am today
without your friendship, guidance, support, and
incredible wealth of knowledge.

Contents

Illustrations

Figures

Tables

Forms and Checklists

RtI Classroom Observations 91

Provides a format for collecting observational data to be used for analyzing instruction design, curriculum, task, and environment as a fidelity check for identified struggling learners. *When to use:* Four weeks into Tier 1 interventions (after student is identified through universal screening); in Tiers 2 and 3, suggested use is twice in each tier (at beginning of tier and at 6 weeks).

RtI Documentation of Tier 1 Instructional Interventions
(Basic Reading, Reading Literacy, Written Language, Math) 92

Organizes documentation of interventions initiated to promote learning and ensures fidelity of implementation. *When to use:* Beginning in Tier 1 (after struggling learner is identified through universal screening).

RtI Documentation: Tier 2/Tier 3 Intervention and Assessment 96

Tracks correct documentation of interventions added in Tiers 2 and 3 to promote learning and ensures fidelity of implementation. *When to use:* Throughout intervention phases in Tiers 2 and 3.

Foreword

The illiterate of the 21st century will not be those who cannot read and write, but those who cannot learn, unlearn, and relearn.

—ALVIN TOFFLER

The fundamental mission of every school should be to guarantee each student learns the skills and knowledge needed to be a self-sufficient, successful adult. All parents hope that schools will prepare their children to become intelligent, responsible adults who possess the knowledge and good character skills to live a happy, successful, satisfying life. That brings us to the question addressed in this book: Why should a school implement Response to Intervention (RtI) or redesign its current RtI process?

The RtI approach holds the promise of ensuring that all children have access to high-quality instruction, and that struggling learners—including those with learning disabilities—are identified, supported, and served early and effectively. When each student has guaranteed access to a rigorous, scientifically valid curriculum with effective high-quality instruction, research-based and targeted early interventions, and intensive support from highly trained educators, failure to learn will be reduced.

Even before the Individuals with Disabilities Education Improvement Act (IDEA) was reauthorized in 2004, instructional leaders (including myself) sensed that the "wait to fail" model was itself failing; it was not providing students with the quality interventions that they needed, when they needed them. A different system, however, *was* working; by focusing on providing quality interventions within the regular education environment, "child-find" was bringing evidence-based practice into the schools. Those educators were proactively finding students who were struggling and then focusing on providing quality interventions within their regular education environment. This was the beginning of a movement in public schools to address students' needs early, and it led to the birth of Response to Intervention.

As a former special education teacher, I was excited by the opportunity to witness this change in philosophy. I agreed with the movement to bring evidence-based practice into education. Our schools should be providing the right intervention as soon as a student starts to fall behind; we should not wait for the gap to grow so wide that a student must qualify for special education before we can provide more help. At the time, I knew the change in philosophy would be difficult, but I also believed it was well worth it. After all, isn't this why we choose to work in education? To help students be the best that they can be!

The task was daunting: to develop a plan to implement RtI, at the same time making sure everyone understood why RtI was important, and to keep everyone excited about this new approach. This was an opportunity to address a student's learning gap in regular education before the gap became so large that the student might never close it. The fundamental premise is that educators should not wait until students fall far enough behind to qualify for special education to provide them with the help they need. Instead, schools should provide *each* student with targeted and systematic help as soon as he or she demonstrates a need.

I was introduced to RtI when I heard about a series of learning opportunities being offered at the Educational Service Center in my area. Dr. Andrea Ogonosky, an educational consultant and school psychologist, was the expert who would share her experience and teach those who were willing to implement this new process in their districts. She conducted the first RtI professional development presentation I attended. I was amazed at our training. Dr. Ogonosky was saying everything I believed! It was evident that Dr. Ogonosky had spent many years researching, developing, and refining the RtI process. She seemed to have this journey completely mapped, to guide us through a lot of networking as we discovered how we could do this. It was almost overwhelming, but that did not matter to me. We were going to ensure that students' needs were addressed early, and that's what counted.

As I collaborated with the professionals in my district who were working to implement RtI (with fidelity!, as we say), I began to correspond with Dr. Ogonosky. Her positive manner guided us and assured us that we were on the right track. Her calmness kept all of us focused on the work of designing learning opportunities that met the needs of our students. She never tired of answering questions during trainings, via email, text, or phone calls. Since then, I have invited Dr. Ogonosky to work with teams implementing RtI in four different districts, from a small district of 1,600 students with very limited resources to a large district of more than 40,000 students and growing. She has developed a system for implementing RtI that works and can be applied in any size district with the resources available. In each district, the common themes I have witnessed are:

- Dr. Ogonosky makes the team feel like we are on the right track.
- Our team is being successful; we can do this.
- Our students' needs are being met.

- We are working too hard (worried about paperwork).
- We understand the urgency of our work.
- We do not want a single child to fail.
- When a student struggles, we focus our attention on finding better ways to meet the student's specific learning needs.

I have also found that it is critical that RtI be overtly supported by the leadership at the district and campus levels, and that the step-by-step guidance provided by Dr. Ogonosky in implementing RtI allows schools to revamp an existing RtI process to be more efficient with less paperwork.

In this second edition of *The Response to Intervention Handbook,* Dr. Ogonosky shares her vast experience in helping educators in school districts achieve extraordinary results through RtI. The book guides administrators and teachers through a seamless three-tier process that is timely and cost efficient. The book will also help parents and educational leaders or specialists understand their roles in the process. Through my experiences, this book is a must.

Over the years, RtI has come to be recognized as an effective system for improving academic and behavioral outcomes for all students. Its foundation is a multi-tier framework approach to the early identification and support of students with learning and/or behavior needs. The RtI process begins with high-quality best practices, research-based instruction, and universal screening of all children in the general education classroom. The system provides research-based targeted intervention immediately upon receiving evidence of a student need. Struggling learners are provided with interventions at increasing levels of intensity to accelerate their rate of learning. Progress is closely monitored to assess both the learning rate and level of performance of individual students. Educational decisions about the intensity and duration of interventions are based on individual student response to scientific, research-based intervention and instruction as part of the evaluation procedures.

The primary purpose of RtI is early intervention to prevent long-term academic failure. Struggling students are identified using data-based progress monitoring and are provided intensive instruction. Use of a scientifically valid curriculum, along with best-practice research-based instructional methods, leads to school improvement. We must deliver high-quality instruction and research-based interventions aligned with individual student need, monitor progress, and use the data to make educational decisions.

Knowing that students learn at different rates, with various learning styles and instructional needs, why would you not implement RtI in your school? Why are we implementing Response to Intervention? For the same reason that we became educators: to help students!

ROBIN PEREZ, ED.D.

SUPERINTENDENT, NEDERLAND ISD

Acknowledgments

As I pondered the decision to revise and update this first book in the RtI Handbook series, I was excited and a little stressed, knowing by now the effort this undertaking would require. As usual my husband, James, has been supportive and encouraging, demonstrating the patience of a saint. James has not wavered in his love for me and support of my dreams! My beautiful daughters, Kim and Emily, and their new husbands, Jon and Danny, inspire me every day. My mom, Aunt Pauline, sisters, and brother are always just a phone call away.

I would also like to acknowledge the many educators I have had the privilege to work with over the past 10 years, designing and implementing RtI systems in schools. Thank you to Dr. Robin Perez, for taking me on four separate journeys and for all I have learned from her leadership. I am also grateful to Karen Mintsioulis, with whom I am looking forward to writing another behavior book. Patti Young and the staff of Weatherford ISD have become very dear to me as we have navigated systems of supports for their children. I learned so much working with Kathy Krenek and her staff in Huffman ISD as well as Mary Jane Bowman and Eileen Littel in Grand Prairie ISD. There are many more who have left an impression on my mind and heart as we continue to advocate for the best education our children deserve. Thank you!

Introduction

Response to Intervention, or RtI, is an approach to general education that is designed to support all students who are struggling both academically and behaviorally. Each of the three tiers in the RtI model represents particular methods of assessment, instructional strategies, and interventions targeted to the struggling learner's needs. The interventions are unique to the needs of the individual student as determined through campus team collaboration and conversations.

This educational approach encourages data-based problem solving for students who are demonstrating difficulty with learning or with social or emotional behavior concerns. The goal of RtI is to improve academic outcomes for all students by intervening early when any student shows signs that he or she is struggling. Data are gathered so that instruction is matched to the individual student and so that research-based interventions focus on the unique needs of the struggling learner. The student's progress—that is, his or her response to the interventions—is monitored and is used in making decisions about strategies for the student's success.

In 2001, the Learning Disabilities Summit, sponsored by the U.S. Department of Education, endorsed RtI's use for identifying learning disabilities. The subsequent passage of both the No Child Left Behind Act of 2001 and the Individuals with Disabilities Education Improvement Act of 2004 (IDEA) propelled RtI onto a national level in the field of education. Over the years, school districts have been navigating through No Child Left Behind, IDEA, and, more recently, the Every Student Succeeds Act (ESSA, the reauthorization of the Elementary and Secondary Education Act). Signed by President Obama on December 10, 2015, ESSA expanded accountability for school improvement and increasing student progress, including those who struggle to master basic skills in reading and mathematics. Since then, RtI has become more of a mainstream part of the educational process; however, there continue to be misunderstandings.

Sustaining the Process

When the first edition of this book was produced 10 years ago, RtI was a relatively new concept being introduced to administrators and teachers. Therefore, the book was designed to help them implement RtI in a practical way, starting with conceptualizing the primary features of the process. This new edition has been revised to provide additional insight into RtI, which has not changed in theory since its original design. New examples and further clarification have been added to help districts work to build and to *sustain* the process. Unfortunately, often the strength of the process relies on one individual person leading the district or campus RtI conversations and is not dependent on a systemic approach to solving problems. When there is inconsistency and the support process is not aligned horizontally (across all the campuses in a district) and vertically (in grades K–12 and all district programs), RtI becomes fractured and ineffective. Ideally, the process is sustained by support from the district administrative level. Sustainability depends on the resources committed to the process and the professional development and coaching provided to campus teams.

On the campus level, the process needs to be integrated into teacher planning teams, since Tier 1 discussions are essential to provide the instructional foundation necessary for all students. As I have reported to hundreds of campuses, Tier 1 conversations are often the most difficult part of the RtI process. Tiers 2 and 3 provide support for individual students at their determined instructional level that is essential to build the foundational skills necessary for success in Tier 1. Remember, Tiers 2 and 3 are in addition to Tier 1. Therefore, the bulk of sustainability and integrity of instruction often occurs during those Tier 1 discussions.

Additionally, to build a strong sustainable system, there needs to be a reasonable time frame for building the strength of each tier. If the district moves too fast, without establishing the necessary components, frustration will be a certainty. Begin by honestly self-assessing current processes, including data collection, instructional and curriculum needs within Tier 1, and additional resources needed for Tiers 2 and 3. Remember to include parents in the conversations, and emphasize the importance of progress monitoring. Build in your professional development plans, and be sure to be selective when choosing members of the campus teams.

As I have worked with campus administrators, staff, and parents, I have seen extraordinary successes with RtI. I have witnessed growth in teacher confidence and skills due to increased staff development opportunities, and growth in student motivation that is directly tied to self-monitoring and awareness of the slightest skill development. For example, one second-grader demonstrated his ability to use collected data to come up with additional interventions that led to continued gains in his reading fluency. He also asked the RtI team for tutoring from a high school buddy when his mother began working at night and could not read with him on a daily basis as planned.

In many of the districts I have worked with during the past 10 years, RtI has made significant positive differences in building the capacity for student growth within all three tiers. Be patient, regroup when you need to, and always plan to self-assess continuously, at each tier, to evaluate what is working. All children deserve the chance to learn, and all educators have the power to provide that chance. Response to Intervention is the process that allows us to do so.

Using This Book

The chapters that follow describe Response to Intervention in detail. Chapter 1 introduces the theory behind the process and the underlying philosophy regarding data-based decision making. Chapter 2 is a guide to laying the foundations for implementing and sustaining RtI successfully. Chapter 3 defines the first tier of RtI in practical terms, focusing on the importance of universal data collection and interventions. The journey into the RtI process continues in Chapter 4, which defines the second tier of support and data collection. Chapter 5 covers the most intensive phase of RtI and offers insight for developing the necessary supports for successful problem solving and outcomes.

RtI involves assessment and both academic and behavioral interventions, and each of these aspects of RtI is carried out in a three-tier flow. The unified RtI process can be envisioned as three sides of a tetrahedron:

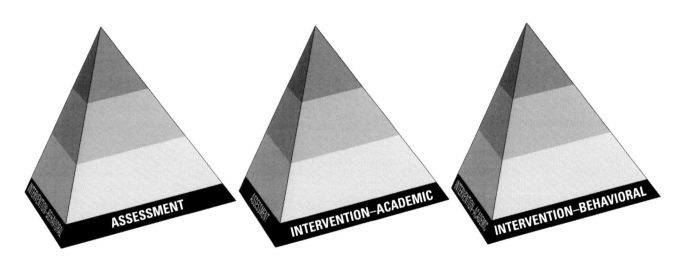

These illustrations are used throughout the book, with the RtI aspect and tier under discussion highlighted so that their place in the unified RtI process can be comprehended in a glance.

Embedded in the chapters are "Lessons Learned" sections to help connect the theory presented to real-life examples of successes (and missteps to avoid). These lessons are based on my experiences from consulting in school districts in Texas, Nevada, Colorado, New York, Florida, New Mexico, Arizona, Rhode Island, Arkansas, and Pennsylvania. All of these districts and their campuses are learning daily, just as yours will be. Some of these lessons are more challenging than others, but I encourage you to regard them all as guides for your own growth and success with RtI.

Appendix A contains answers to a range of questions I am often asked when consulting with school districts about RtI. A collection of forms for RtI team documentation is included in Appendix B; and Appendix C is a handy list of online resources that are most helpful in guiding a district as it develops and implements its own RtI process. Guides to the use of multiple sources of data are presented in Appendix D, followed by the RIOT/ICEL framework for organizing data sources in Appendix E. At the back of the book are a glossary of terms related to the RtI process, a list of abbreviations used in the text, and a bibliography of useful references.

A variety of useful forms and documents detailing data, problem solving, and processes are provided within this book. These documents are meant to be examples of how to integrate information and develop parameters for transitioning into RtI, as well as to emphasize the importance of data collection. Digital versions of the forms and documents may be downloaded from http://ed311. com/ertiforms/. They include checklists and worksheets (organized by RtI tier) for district-wide planning of assessments and interventions, criteria for scientific-based research, and observation of instructional strategies. Although these documents are copyrighted, the copyright is waived for educational support use by purchasers of this book.

Chapter 1

Understanding "Response to Intervention"

Response to Intervention (RtI) is an ongoing process that will need continual revisions as the district systems for instruction and curriculum evolve yearly. Many districts have implemented parts of this system for the past several years. In RtI, however, there is a major shift in responsibility for struggling learners—from special education to the general education classroom. View RtI as a seamless problem-solving process that enhances the learning of *all* children by using consultation and support among *all* educators, combining the unique talents of both general educators and specialists. With RtI, high-quality instruction is matched to student needs by using frequent data collection to guide all decisions regarding student progress.

struggling learners Students with characteristics that indicate they have a higher chance of failing in the areas of learning and behavior.

This process should look very familiar to teachers because they already use this approach informally on a regular basis. RtI simply formalizes this problem-solving method. When educators shift their mind-set and come to view all professionals on campus—general and special educators alike—as available for consultation and support for all children, great things can happen. Teachers begin to feel empowered to tap into resources they previously believed were available only if the student had been given a "label" for services; parents become active partners in intervention support; and students take ownership of their learning.

Features of a Sustainable Problem-Solving Process

The core characteristics of the RtI model have been described by the National Association of State Directors of Special Education (NASDSE 2005) and can be summarized as follows:

sustainable problem-solving process A set of principles and procedures that guide instruction and intervention in ways that can be maintained and defended over time.

RtI model A conception of the process known as Response to Intervention for delivering scientifically based instruction and interventions to facilitate student learning.

- **All children can be taught** using high-quality instruction in the general education setting. This belief is communicated daily in schools across America with the slogan commonly displayed on doors and windows: "All children can learn."

intervention Any process that has the effect of increasing learning or modifying a student's behavior.

universal strategies Instructional and behavioral strategies that are available to all students.

research-based strategies Instructional designs and recommendations that have been demonstrated through formal scientific research to improve learning.

tiers of intervention Levels of increasingly intense interventions to help students learn.

problem-solving method A set of specific steps for solving problems related to the challenging aspects of teaching and learning.

curriculum The set of courses, coursework, and content offered at a school.

fidelity The degree to which something is carried out as designed, intended, or planned.

assessment The process of using evaluation tools to gather and analyze information about student skill level and progress and the effectiveness of curricula and teaching methods.

screening A type of assessment used to predict which students are likely to experience difficulty learning.

diagnostics A precise form of assessment that analyzes individual student strengths and weaknesses.

progress monitoring Frequent measurement of student progress in a brief, repeatable, reliable, and scientifically valid way; usually performed at predetermined intervals to allow for timely modification of instructional design to suit the student's needs.

- **Intervention occurs early,** when learning and behavior problems are small. It is far easier (and more effective) to intervene using **universal, research-based strategies** when a problem is first developing than to wait until larger deficits require more intense forms of intervention.

- To meet the instructional and behavioral needs of students, applying graduated levels of interventions, or **tiers of interventions,** is crucial. **Tier 1** applies to all students, and **Tiers 2 and 3** apply to students who need greater levels of intervention. The multi-tier approach helps campus support teams tailor their instruction and services to struggling learners.

- Within the multi-tier model, the **problem-solving method** has been highly effective in helping to clearly define student needs and to match those needs to instructional strategies and interventions. Using this method for making decisions includes asking a hierarchy of questions whose answers are driven by data:

  1. Is there a problem? If so, what is it, and why is it happening?
  2. How can we use the curriculum to solve the problem?
  3. What interventions can we use to solve the problem? How can we implement them?
  4. Did the interventions work? Or do we need to try something else?

  In RtI, this problem-solving approach is applied to *all* students within *all* tiers.

- **Interventions and curricula are based on research** and are scientifically validated, as required by the Elementary and Secondary Education Act (ESEA) and the Individuals with Disabilities Education Improvement Act (IDEA).

- **Student progress is monitored** by frequently collecting data to determine the effectiveness of interventions that have been implemented. The data are directly related to the curriculum that has been introduced, and they are sensitive to the slightest skill development.

- **All decisions are data-based.** This is a critical feature and the one that is probably the most difficult to implement with **fidelity.** This feature requires that all systems for ongoing assessment be in place.

- Decisions are driven by all of the data gathered from **assessment** within each tier. Assessment tools are used for the **screening of all students (Tier 1)** to determine which ones are not making the same academic and behavioral gains as their peers; for **diagnostics (Tiers 1 and 2)** to determine which students are unable to demonstrate essential academic and behavioral skills; and for **progress monitoring (Tiers 2 and 3)** to guide decision making about interventions.

A Three-Tier Approach

RtI focuses on delivering high-quality instruction and interventions based on data that document learning rates and levels of performance. These data guide the RtI team in making important decisions about the intensity and duration of interventions for individual students. The core components of RtI are multiple tiers of interventions, high-quality instruction based on scientific research, data-based decision making, and research-based interventions.

Much has already been written about the current "wait-to-fail" model that prompted the President's Commission on Excellence in Education and IDEA to promote early intervention. In RtI, district resources are arranged to provide a unified system of education that incorporates early intervention. To accomplish this process in your district, your general education and special education systems must be unified.

The starting place is to recognize several important characteristics of RtI. First, RtI is not a special education initiative, although most district personnel have been interpreting it that way. Additionally, under RtI, a child does not need an eligibility condition, or "label," to receive individualized support. And finally, procedural guidelines to frame the process and guide continuous improvement must be in place at both the district and campus levels.

RtI problem solving emphasizes assessment as the foundation for making decisions and for monitoring instructional effectiveness. This assessment provides the data for structured problem solving. Within that decision-making process, team members must be flexible as they identify which resources are already available and which additional resources are needed to support learning.

There are many variations of the tiered model of RtI. The three major components of this approach are often described in words (table 1.1) and can also be conceptualized visually, with the major components forming three sides of a tiered tetrahedron (figures 1.1–1.3; details presented in these figures and in table 1.1 are discussed in depth in Chapters 3–5). Often the three-tier model indicates increasingly intense levels of intervention, applied to decreasing numbers of students (table 1.2 and figure 1.4). All students receive Tier 1 interventions, regardless of any other tiers of intervention that may be occurring for individual students. Likewise, students who move from Tier 2 to Tier 3 will receive intensified Tier 2 interventions. Some districts have proposed a fourth tier in their model; in that case, Tier 3 remains within the regular education domain, and Tier 4 indicates a formal referral to special education. In this book, as in most tiered RtI models, special education is encompassed in Tier 3.

instruction The act of delivering information so that learning can occur.

learning rate The pace of a student's skill acquisition; one of the elements used for making decisions in RtI.

performance Measurable outcomes that are characteristic of student learning.

eligibility conditions Conditions defined by federal and state governments for determining whether children qualify to receive special education services.

Table 1.1. Elements of a three-tier RtI approach

RtI Components by Tier	Description	Procedures for Implementation
TIER 1 • Universal screening • Diagnostics • Progress monitoring *High-quality instructional and behavioral supports are provided for all students in general education.*	• Collection and sharing of benchmark data among teachers, principals, district staff, and parents (data are collected in fall, winter, and spring) • Specific, objective measures of problem areas, not anecdotal information or opinions	• School personnel conduct universal screening of academic and behavioral skills. • Teachers implement a variety of research-supported instructional strategies. • Ongoing curriculum-based assessment (continuous progress monitoring) is used to guide high-quality instruction. • Students receive differentiated instruction based on data from ongoing assessments.
TIER 2 • Baseline data collection • Diagnostics • Progress monitoring • Written plan of accountability • Comparison of pre- and post-intervention data *Students whose performance and rate of progress lag behind those of peers in their classroom, school, or district receive more-specialized prevention or remediation within general education.*	• Curriculum-based measurement (CBM) to determine whether a problem area is an issue with the student or the core curriculum • Which interventions will be tried that are different? Who will do them? When? Where? For how long? • Frequent collection of a variety of data to examine student performance over time and evaluate interventions in order to make data-based decisions • Data-based decision making for intervention effectiveness	• Curriculum-based measures are used to identify which students continue to need assistance with specific kinds of skills. • Collaborative problem solving is used to design and implement instructional support for students that may consist of more-individualized strategies and interventions. • Student progress is monitored frequently to determine intervention effectiveness. • Systematic assessment is conducted to determine the fidelity with which instruction and interventions are implemented. • Parents are informed and are involved in planning. • General education teachers receive support (training, consultation, direct services).
TIER 3 • Increased intensity of interventions *Tier 3 includes all the elements of Tier 2. The difference between Tier 2 and Tier 3 is the frequency and group size of the intervention treatment.*	• The most intensive phase of RtI • Fidelity of intervention ensured by documentation • If progress monitoring does not establish improvement after intervention phase is implemented, referral for multidisciplinary assessment for special education is warranted.	• Procedures are consistent with those of Tier 2. • Intensity of interventions increases; treatment time and group size vary with intervention.

Source: Adapted from a chart developed by Andrea Ogonosky, Gail Cheramie, and Carol Booth, 2006.

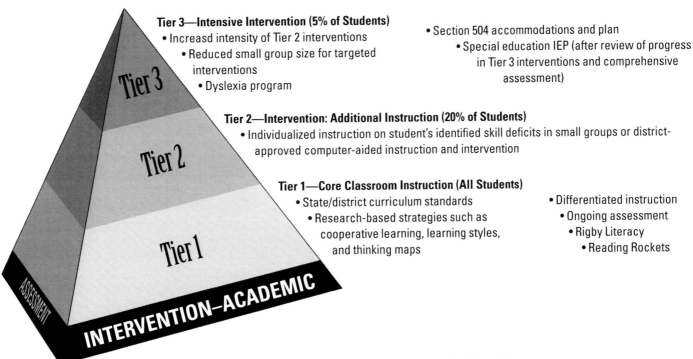

Tier 3—Progress Monitoring; Comprehensive Assessments
- Universal screening
- District benchmark assessment(s)
- Instructional assessments
- Curriculum-based measurements (3 times per week)
- Dyslexia assessment
- Full and individual evaluation

Tier 2—Progress Monitoring; District and Classroom Assessments
- Universal screening
- District benchmark assessment(s)
- Instructional assessments
- Baseline curriculum-based measurement
- Curriculum-based measurements (2 times per week)

Tier 1—Universal Screening; State, District, and Classroom Assessments
- Curriculum-based measurement (3 times per year)
- District benchmark assessments
- Norm-referenced assessments (3 times per year)
- Instructional assessments

INTERVENTION–BEHAVIORAL

ASSESSMENT

Figure 1.1. Example of district-wide assessments in the three-tier RtI model.

Tier 3—Intensive Intervention (5% of Students)
- Increasd intensity of Tier 2 interventions
- Reduced small group size for targeted interventions
- Dyslexia program
- Section 504 accommodations and plan
- Special education IEP (after review of progress in Tier 3 interventions and comprehensive assessment)

Tier 2—Intervention: Additional Instruction (20% of Students)
- Individualized instruction on student's identified skill deficits in small groups or district-approved computer-aided instruction and intervention

Tier 1—Core Classroom Instruction (All Students)
- State/district curriculum standards
- Research-based strategies such as cooperative learning, learning styles, and thinking maps
- Differentiated instruction
- Ongoing assessment
- Rigby Literacy
- Reading Rockets

ASSESSMENT

INTERVENTION–ACADEMIC

Figure 1.2. Example of district-wide academic interventions in the three-tier RtI model.

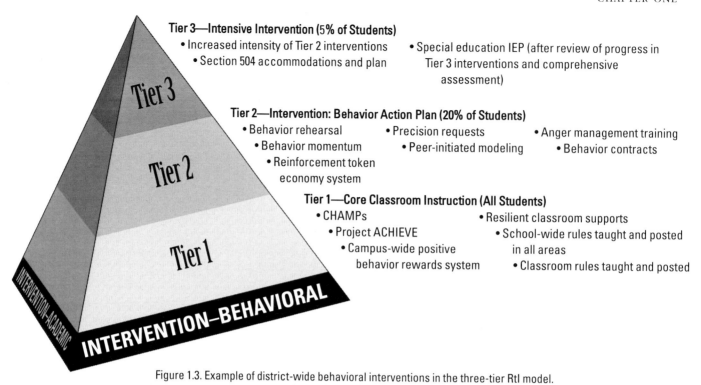

Figure 1.3. Example of district-wide behavioral interventions in the three-tier RtI model.

Table 1.2. Levels of intervention and assessment in the three–tier RtI model

Tier 1 (100% of students)	Tier 2 (about 20% of students)	Tier 3 (about 5% of students)
• High-quality instruction and behavioral supports for all students • Decision making based on universal screening and benchmarking *Approximately 80% of students receive only Tier 1 interventions and assessments. The remaining students will also receive Tier 2, and some of those will also receive Tier 3.*	• Targeted interventions • Progress monitoring (CBM) to inform decisions *Approximately 15% of students receive only Tier 1 and Tier 2 interventions and assessments. The remaining 5% will also receive Tier 3.*	• Increased intensity of targeted interventions • Continued progress monitoring • Possible referral to special education

RtI: Problem Solving

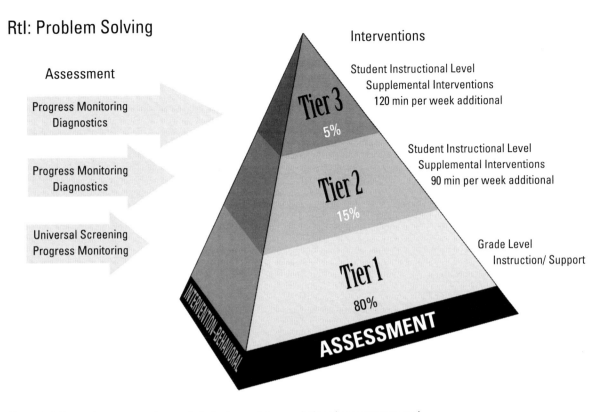

Figure 1.4. Approximate percentages of students receiving each tier of assessments and interventions. All students receive Tier 1 assessments and interventions. A portion of students also receive Tier 2 assessments and interventions, and a small percentage receive all three tiers.

Data-Based Problem Solving

Problem solving in RtI is completely data driven. Teachers routinely collect data in the form of observations, criterion-referenced testing, and student products. The discussion happens for Tier 1 during planning by the professional learning community and for Tiers 2 and 3 during the decision point problem-solving meeting of the RtI campus team. Typically, staff tend to make decisions based on emotions and not on collected data. RtI data collection focuses on student foundational skill needs and projected learning rates, which can then be directly linked to intervention effectiveness (thus removing the subjective factor).

criterion-referenced assessment A measure of performance in terms of a clearly defined learning task.

student product Something created by a student to demonstrate learning of a skill.

professional learning community A group of teachers in a grade-level or content area who meet regularly and work collaboratively to improve their teaching skills and the academic performance of students.

Lessons Learned: When campus problem-solving teams focus on Tier 1 instructional strategies, such as differentiated instruction and scaffolding within small group instruction, amazing growth can occur. One campus team reported that before their campus-based RtI team process was initiated, 65 percent of the team's first-grade students were not proficient in fluency of letter identification at the beginning of the school year. They also indicated that approximately 45 of their 125 students were identified as ready to begin a Tier 2 intervention. The team reflected during year 1 of the RtI process that they were focusing on the wrong strategies and wanted to jump too quickly into individualized interventions, when in fact they needed to discuss Tier 1 teaching strategies and have a plan to work collaboratively with kindergarten teachers on increasing the effectiveness of Tier 1, particularly for their English language learners who were continually struggling as an identified subpopulation. Once the discussions began, major changes were made to the structure of small group instruction and guided reading groups within the first grade. Additional supports were provided to the kindergarten teachers as well, in the form of curriculum resources and training on strategies for English language learners. Year 2 of the process yielded positive trends in closing the reading gaps for the kindergarten and first-grade students.

The rewards for using a systematic problem-solving process are that resources for students are used more flexibly; parents become more involved; interventions are implemented within the general education setting, with supports from additional staff (school psychologists, speech and language pathologists, physical therapists, social workers); and student achievement increases.

Chapter 2

Implementing RtI

stablishing or reenergizing Response to Intervention in your school system will require changes in your structural and cultural organization, beginning with defining the primary roles and responsibilities of all staff and of parents. Campus administrators must embrace the problem-solving approach of RtI before attempting to carry out the process. Along with promoting change, leadership in the transition becomes a key element in the success of implementation. Campus and district administrators must understand the thought process of using this system as it relates to expectations. For starters, the Every Student Succeeds Act (ESSA) states that "schools, local education agencies, and States" must be held "accountable for improving the academic achievement of *all* students" and "promoting schoolwide reform and ensuring the access of *all* children to effective, scientifically-based instructional strategies."

Promoting the Philosophy of RtI

In his book *Failing Forward: Turning Mistakes into Stepping Stones for Success,* John C. Maxwell (2000) identified four factors to promote success when leading an organization through change. To achieve success in implementing RtI, the administrator must first focus on the **relationships** that have been developed with staff and parents. These relationships will affect every aspect of decision making along the way. The next factor is to have **big dreams.** All effective leaders can achieve a vision with the right team, but how high the team will soar depends on the **attitude** the leader brings to the change process. Lastly, every outcome will be the result of the personal **leadership skills** the administrator possesses. Therefore, continued personal and professional growth should be nonnegotiable, particularly when it comes to understanding and committing to the concepts of RtI. The most effective leaders of RtI have embraced change and observed the incredible positive aspects of supporting all students and meeting their needs, not with a labeling system, but through a seamless process that acknowledges all types of learners using strong data to drive the decisions.

What is most important in helping school staff and parents trust the problem-solving process of RtI is to continue to make the necessary supports available every year for a successful implementation of the intervention and instruction programs. From the start, all administrators must actively and publicly support the RtI process.

According to Sylvia Méndez-Morse (1992), effective leaders of change have some characteristics in common. Leadership begins with a vision that is developed and shared. The leaders in education who have been able to accomplish great changes are those who were proactive and took risks. They were able to recognize the evolving needs of the staff and parents, to anticipate necessary changes, and to effectively challenge the notion of "status quo." Additionally, an administrator's abilities both to communicate and to listen influence the shift in philosophy significantly.

Several barriers will present themselves at this time of change. For example, campus leaders will need to identify which interventions currently being used on the campus are effective for struggling learners. They must then analyze those interventions; decide whether the interventions are research-based, as defined by ESSA and the Individuals with Disabilities Education Improvement Act; and set the expectation that all personnel will implement the interventions with fidelity. As administrators provide continuous monitoring and evaluation, they will face barriers from those who are resisting the change or are having difficulty understanding it. Commonly, statements such as these are heard during RtI policy training on campus at the beginning of the year: "I have so many students in my class that I cannot possibly do this"; "Where is special education? This is really their issue"; and "I have tried everything I know. This cannot be a problem with the curriculum or instruction—it surely must be a problem with the child." One of the biggest challenges for all administrators is to help their educators understand that RtI is not merely a referral process to special education; rather, it is a process that focuses on high-quality instructional practices and research-based interventions to support the struggling learner. RtI is not a vehicle on the road to special education—it is a journey of interventions to support learning. To reenergize your current process and prevent drifting from this message, be sure that administrators, team members, and teachers are given professional growth opportunities every year on RtI problem-solving strategies.

Lessons Learned: Understanding that the change process will take time is extremely important. Implementing RtI does not happen overnight—it will take several years to develop. Patience and flexibility are the keys to success. How much time? If policies and resources are established, the process of implementing a sustainable change will take three to five years. Additionally, there should be an expectation that this process will grow and develop as the school district grows. Therefore, when adjustments need to be made, they will not be viewed as a negative but instead will reflect the ongoing positive changes in resources and support that the district deems necessary.

Setting Up a Sustainable Process

A major concern in the public school system is to help struggling learners progress at an acceptable rate in the general education grade-level curriculum. Parents and staff become very frustrated when a child falls behind in learning to read, write, or do math. Response to Intervention conversations around data are essential to making accurate decisions about the effectiveness of general and additional skill-based remedial instruction. RtI promotes the notion that how well a subject is taught gauges how well students learn. In the purest form, RtI is simply about personalizing information for individual students to promote their academic success. The intent of the process is to decrease the number of "curriculum casualties" by ensuring that all students are given high-quality instruction with fidelity. It is an opportunity for educators to resolve students' learning difficulties by primarily focusing on student needs and not on special education eligibility decisions. RtI is about what will be done rather than where it will be done, and how to intervene as opposed to who will do the intervention.

Once district administrators have defined their expectations for RtI, the campus administrator needs to meet with grade-level teams to discuss assessment methods and resources currently being used for implementing RtI. Information gathered will focus on how teachers and instructional specialists/interventionists are addressing the specific needs for each student identified within each tier of the process. The following steps need to be taken during the transition to RtI:

1. Review and determine fidelity of existing assessment structure: current district benchmarks, state-mandated testing, assessments to identify students who may need specialized programs, and teacher data collection (student products, district-required standardized assessments, pre-referral assessments, special education assessment practices). ***District and campus level***

2. Check for alignment of assessment tools with curriculum. Which of the current assessments measure whether the student is learning what is expected? ***District and campus level***

3. Develop yearly training on selected universal screening measures and publish the district's selected dates of administration (three times per year, in the fall, winter, and spring). ***District level (to ensure consistency across campuses)***

standardized assessment A type of test that is developed according to standard procedures and is administered and scored in a consistent manner for all students.

pre-referral assessment An evaluation of whether further assessment is needed to determine a student's special education eligibility. This type of assessment does not focus on developing intervention strategies.

align To reorganize and modify components as needed so that they form a unified system.

4. Use the district's identified database system for documenting and interpreting results from universal screening. ***District level***

5. Use guidelines for interpreting multiple data sources for decision making (figure 2.1). Review existing district documentation forms and use them to document the campus decision making within the RtI process. ***District level***

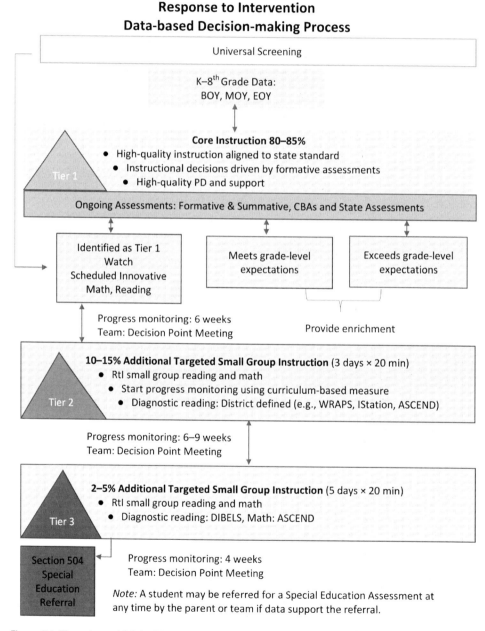

Figure 2.1. Flow chart of RtI decision making based on multiple data sources.

Once administrators and staff understand the district's expectations for intervening with struggling learners—particularly the way in which the campuses will now evaluate individual student progress—then district *and* campus administrators must work together to create a solid foundation necessary for sustaining the RtI problem-solving process. The district should develop comprehensive guidelines for implementation, including how current campus assessment tools will be inventoried and how existing pre-referral and intervention practices will be evaluated (figure 2.2). At this stage, administrators need to focus on campus leadership (knowledge and skills), existing intervention teams, core curriculum, current screening procedures, and needs for professional development. To fully embrace the RtI process, the school district must expand its comprehensive plans to incorporate sustainable policies and procedures for consistency over time of the conversations and data collection necessary for continued success.

Lessons Learned: To ensure a sustainable system, the campus administrator must engage and interact with district-level committees and department leaders to commit campus resources to a system that has the following components:

- Multiple tiers of instruction and assessment
- Use of data: balanced assessments that are supported by the district and campus
- Technology for ease of documentation and progress monitoring
- Highly qualified staff (instruction and assessment throughout all three tiers)

Evaluating Where You Are

Before you reboot and reenergize your RtI process, it would be wise to begin with several planning meetings (at least two to four) at the district administrative level. Attendees should include the superintendent and assistant superintendent(s), curriculum coordinators (elementary and secondary), special education administrators, reading and math intervention coordinators, the district at-risk coordinator for Section 504, the counseling coordinator, and parent liaisons.

The agenda of the meetings should focus on training the attendees in understanding the district philosophy and expectations for RtI, what ESSA and IDEA mean when they refer to research-based instructional practices and interventions, and the roles of general education staff, special education staff, and parent involvement. Plan to use the remaining meetings to discuss and realign the

Section 504 Part of the federal Rehabilitation Act of 1973 that protects individuals with disabilities against discrimination. The civil rights of students in school settings are protected under Section 504, which requires a school district to provide a "free appropriate public education" (FAPE) to each qualified student with a disability who is in the school district's jurisdiction, regardless of the nature or severity of the disability. Regular or special education and related aids and services must be designed to meet the student's individual educational needs as adequately as the needs of nondisabled students are met.

Response to Intervention Framework

MISSION STATEMENT: School District purpose, in partnership with families and community, is to develop life-long learners intellectually, emotionally, physically, and socially who are complex thinkers, responsible global citizens and effective communicators.

VISION STATEMENT: We believe that character and community values are essential for building responsible citizens. We also believe that accountability coupled with high expectations should be expected from all staff and students. We also believe that all graduates must be challenged and equipped to succeed in the 21st century.

Response to Intervention, or RtI, is the practice of meeting the academic and behavioral needs of all students through problem-solving with three key elements:

- High-quality instruction and research-based tiered interventions aligned with identified individual needs based on student data.
- Frequent monitoring of student progress to enable results-based academic and/or behavioral decisions.
- Use of student response data in making important educational decisions, such as those regarding placement, intervention, curriculum, and instructional goals and methodologies.

The instructional approaches within the general education setting should result in academic and/or behavioral progress for students within the general education curriculum. Struggling students are identified using data-based measures and are provided intensive instruction. The use of a scientifically validated curriculum, as well as instructional methods expected in an RtI model, leads to student and school improvement.

RtI is the system of providing high-quality instruction and intervention matched to student need, monitoring progress frequently to make decisions about change in instructional goals, and applying the student's response data to important education decisions. The primary focus of RtI is early intervention to prevent long-term academic failure.

Texas SB 1153

SB 1153 requires each school to notify parents, each year, if their child is receiving assistance for learning difficulties, including through "intervention strategies."

The notice must be provided when the child begins to receive the assistance for that year, must be in writing, and must be provided in the parent's native language "to the extent practicable."

The notice must include:

a. A reasonable description of the assistance, including any intervention strategies that may be used;

b. Information collected regarding any intervention in the base tier of a multi-tiered system of supports that has been used;

c. An estimate of the duration for which the assistance will be provided;

d. The estimated time frame for reporting progress on the assistance to the parents; and

e. A copy of the notice to be provided by TEA, which will include notification to parents that they can request an evaluation at any time for services under IDEA or Section 504.

Figure 2.2. Example of a school district's framework of expectations for the RtI process.

The timing of the progress reports will have to be an individualized decision for each student. Many students will have the same, or similar, timeframes for progress reporting; *it will depend on the interventions being used.* As a practical matter, sending progress reports on the RtI services at the same intervals as report cards or IEP progress reports may be the most efficient manner to ensure that the deadlines are remembered and not missed. However, this may be different when required by the specific intervention strategies used.

DISTRICT EXPECTATIONS

- The principal is responsible for the campus-based RtI problem-solving process.
- Each campus will have a RtI team (typically 5 to 7 members)
- The campus RtI team will meet regularly to analyze student data, update progress, and align with state-required RtI intervention plans.
- District Cutoff Score (using campus-chosen instrument) is aligned to national/state recommended cutoff score of the 25th percentile.
- Selected interventions will be implemented and monitored for fidelity.
- Use guidance from SB 1153 (Texas) to communicate the RtI plan/results and progress monitoring with students' parents.

THE BIG 3: GUIDELINES FOR IMPLEMENTATION

I. Data

a) Universal screening 3 times per year (BOY, MOY, EOY) with campus-chosen instrument.

b) Diagnostic data to determine targeted skills

c) Progress monitoring: Tier 1, ongoing with naturally occurring teacher-collected data (grade level)

d) Progress monitoring: Tiers 2 and 3, RtI decision making (communicated to parents in letter format) used for determining movement in Tiers and defining student growth on RtI Plan

II. Intervention

a) Tier 1 identified students: Supportive instructional and learning strategies and tutorials to build grade-level knowledge (aligned to TEKS).

b) Tiers 2 and 3: Foundational skill-specific additional instruction and strategies needed for student to progress and show growth.

III. RtI Plan

a) Goals that are specific and measurable

b) Baseline data specific with expected rate of improvement

c) Defined assessment tool for progress monitoring

d) Defined interval and frequency for collection of progress-monitoring data process and how to integrate current successful practices with the district vision for RtI.

Once the group demonstrates not only an *understanding* but also a *willingness* to move forward, the real planning can begin. Be prepared for initial frustrations and barriers that will surface, as all involved at this level must reevaluate and possibly shift their own philosophies regarding RtI, curriculum, teaching, and intervention. At this level, the main issues to surface initially are related to turfs. Curriculum specialists may become defensive during discussions on evaluating current practices and aligning them with ESSA standards and expectations for the implementation of research-based strategies. Special education personnel may focus on eligibility issues. Reading specialists may home in on resources and preferred individual reading practices.

During these initial planning meetings, persons in authority must be willing to accept adjustments to the current RtI policies and practices. All personnel on the RtI district-level committee will invest time and effort in redesigning and updating procedures and expectations for working with all students. The districts that are the most successful move beyond any resistance to changing the status quo, which can be overwhelming when other initiatives are being introduced within the district at the same time. It is most important to honor all perspectives and not become defensive and entrenched in thinking, "This is how we have always done it."

If there is resistance, it is best to resolve it during these initial meetings at the district administrative level, because the decisions made then will form the perspective that ultimately influences the campus leadership. Stop and take the time to investigate research-based practices currently being used on campuses and to address all concerns at this stage. Although this can be uncomfortable, the benefits of not rushing through this particular stage are significant.

Once the district leadership RtI committee is in agreement on the philosophy and district perspective on RtI, several important tasks must be addressed. This team must prepare guidance for the *ongoing* support of RtI in the district:

1. Discuss how to provide needed staff development. Create a staff development plan that includes training and materials for new and existing staff.
   a. RtI process
   b. ESSA and IDEA regulations
   c. Curriculum and instructional levels of student matched with progress-monitoring assessments in Tiers 2 and 3
   d. Leadership training for all campus administrators
2. Generate district models of assessments, research-based academic interventions, and research-based behavioral interventions (refer to figures 1.1–1.3 for examples).
   a. Develop and describe assessments used for problem solving within the tiers

(see "Using Multiple Sources of Data" in Appendix D)

    b. Align academic and behavioral instruction and identified curriculum or computer-based interventions with the appropriate tiers, according to intervention intensity

    c. Ensure that the assessment tools and interventions identified are available to the RtI team and school staff

3. Review current membership of the campus-based team and identify a core RtI team on each campus; two teams may be necessary on secondary campuses or very large campuses.

    a. Design training for administrators on appropriate team membership and roles

    b. Design *ongoing* training for the campus teams

        i. Procedural guidelines

        ii. Problem-solving process

        iii. Core curriculum standards and assessment of standards

        iv. Tiers of assessment

        v. Tiers of intervention

        vi. Collaboration and critical skill development

4. Review and edit current guidelines for the campus team process.

    a. Generate norms of meetings, including regularly scheduled times (campus consultations or individual student meetings)

    b. Review how parents will be notified and included in the process and establish consistency across the district.

    c. Review and revisit current systems for collection, analysis, and publication of data

    d. Discuss decision points using new or existing data for expectations regarding movement of students between tiers

    e. Develop a guide for expectations of team roles and meeting procedures

        i. Define how data will be examined and discussed

        ii. Prioritize trends and gaps in student achievement and behavioral issues

        iii. Establish an action plan with measurable outcomes and data collection

5. Set up a system for faculty, staff, and parents to communicate with each other about the RtI process.

decision points Guidelines developed by the district for gauging whether a student may need more intensive interventions within the RtI process.

Lessons Learned: In my consultations with several school districts, it became apparent that district-level committee meetings to revisit and plan for continued growth and sustainability should be on the district calendar and should occur quarterly throughout the school year. These meetings should be considered mandatory, with the expectation that all members will be present.

> **Lessons Learned:** District-level expectations and policies need to focus on the following:
>
> - District policies and procedures for RtI framework
> - Structure/definition of the tiered intervention process
> - Alignment of student needs with district-level program access (Section 504, Dyslexia, Special Education Individualized Educational Programs)
> - Policies that define parent notification and involvement
> - Clarification of due process procedural guidelines for Section 504 and special education concerns or issues that may arise

Planning for Ongoing Staff Development

staff development Intensive and ongoing training for teachers, administrators, and educational specialists, with a goal of improving the performance of both staff and students.

In order for RtI to be successful, all staff must understand the district's philosophy regarding the RtI process—and the rationale behind it. According to the National Association of State Directors of Special Education (NASDSE 2005), effective staff development plans should follow standards adopted by the National Staff Development Council (2001). These standards form a strong foundation for designing, implementing, and supporting staff development regarding RtI. They focus on integrating staff development with school improvement data, providing assistance for administrators as they transition from the existing referral process to the supportive RtI process, and evaluating the success of the transition to RtI. For effective staff development, Showers, Joyce, and Bennett (1987) recommend that teaching modules incorporate theory, demonstration, practice, and feedback. To maintain the foundational RtI skills that the staff acquire, practice and feedback are vital, so plan for long-term training and support within the district.

Some specific modules should be incorporated in the planning for staff development. All staff should be instructed on the national and state policies driving RtI, the theory and models of RtI, use of the problem-solving process within both general education and special education, and assessment methods in all three tiers. In addition, plan for modules tailored to the needs of district and campus leaders, as well as campus staff.

The first team meetings of district leaders can cover the three-tier RtI model of assessment methods and interventions, development of training and supports for campus administrators, coordination of district resources for RtI success, and parent involvement.

service delivery model A description of the way in which services—such as classroom placement, strategic interventions, peer tutoring, cooperative grouping, and differentiated instruction—will be provided to students.

For campus administrators, staff development concentrates on the following strands: RtI service delivery, allocation of staff and the budget (how to integrate resources between general and special education), leadership skills necessary for facilitating the change process, recognizing and dismantling resistance and barriers to implementation of RtI, assessing campus readiness, and planning for campus needs.

Staff development at the campus level emphasizes understanding the three-tier model and the district rationale for supporting RtI, research on the need for change and on evidence in support of RtI, training to develop specific skills for various research-based instructional and behavioral strategies within the general education setting (including use of district forms and other documentation, data collection techniques and interpretation of results, and decision making), and the changing roles of personnel as the RtI process is embraced on the campus.

According to NASDSE (2005), a successful staff development plan must address the critical areas of beliefs/attitudes, knowledge level, and skills. The best avenue for designing the staff development needed at each leadership level is the data collected through readiness surveys, which ascertain campus and staff needs. Opportunities for feedback throughout the year are also embedded in the staff development plan, by scheduling practice sessions and by observing the implementation of teaching strategies, interventions, and assessment.

Lessons Learned: Campuses that implement RtI without sufficient time for practice and feedback as part of staff development are not successful in sustaining the conversations necessary for fidelity of all three tiers of instruction and intervention throughout the year. As state assessments loom on the horizon, staff may revert to a reactive, referral-to-test mentality (that is, staff will assume that the student must have a "label" to receive an accommodation or service), which slows the delivery of intervention as well as RtI problem solving. This has yielded an increase in referrals to special education that result in a "Did Not Qualify" (DNQ) decision, leading to frustration of staff and parents and continued failure for the student. It is important to note that once a student is referred for a special education evaluation, two things typically happen:

1. Intervention and instruction taper off during the assessment.
2. The student misses important grade-level content instruction during the evaluation sessions (some may lose up to 10 hours of instruction in new skills).

referral-to-test model A service delivery model in which a student must be referred to a campus team and tested for eligibility before receiving special education supports and services.

Lessons Learned: It is important to create a sustainable system with the culture and climate necessary to support existing and revised RtI expectations and policies. There are 10 essentials:

1. Collaboration among all staff and parents is key to success.
2. Emotions and emotional decision making are left at the door. Data are used for all problem solving.
3. Leadership supports the campus-based process (master scheduling, team selection, budgeting of resources).
4. Teams are essential (never underestimate the power of a strong team to build sustainable student growth).
5. Campus culture affects outcomes and fidelity of the instruction and interventions.
6. It's all about the data (multiple sources, of course).
7. Tier 1 is the first priority of a strong RtI process.
8. Tiers 2/3 are designed to be short-term solutions that bring about long-term results.
9. Documentation is necessary and important to measure growth and intervention effectiveness.
10. All learners, all the time, are on the team radar.

Supporting Intervention Strategies

The district-level committee is responsible for evaluating and defining curriculum and instructional resources that will support campus administrators and staff as they select and are trained in effective intervention strategies to be used within the RtI tiered process. Intervention strategies should be analyzed by the district-level personnel who are most familiar with content and behavioral areas. District-level staff may want to form small committees that will identify intervention strategies currently used within the district and determine ease of access, fidelity of use, and effectiveness, particularly within subpopulations identified as at-risk (for example, English language learners). Things do get very interesting when the committees begin to analyze interventions. Individual campuses may be using strategies that parents have suggested, peers have developed, or teachers have adopted based on personal experience, and these might not meet the state standards for research-based curricula and interventions.

The team needs to evaluate and support or adopt interventions that will be consistently implemented throughout the district. That will enable uniform planning for staff development for teachers and support personnel, as well as provide consistency when a child moves between campuses within the district.

Doing this will also support one very important aspect of RtI: high-quality interventions that are implemented with fidelity and consistency. (For more on this, see "Problem Solving versus Standard Protocol" in Chapter 4.)

Lessons Learned: After inventorying the variety of programs that various campuses in the district have adopted, tread lightly when discussing their effectiveness with campus personnel. One district discovered that a very pricey program a campus had adopted to use for reading interventions did not meet standards suggested by the Florida Center for Reading Research (www.fcrr.org). When the campus administrator was contacted, he reported that the campus PTA had purchased the program. The administrator was concerned that there would be hurt feelings if the organization was told that the program did not meet the district's new standards for research-based interventions. The district-level team then developed an action plan to aid the administrator in dealing with this sensitive issue.

Defining the Team Process

It is crucial that the district train all campus administrators on policy and procedural guidelines; this will provide the structure necessary for consistency and fidelity of the RtI process within and between campuses. These guidelines should cover the following:

- District expectations regarding the RtI process
- The operational definition of the RtI tiers
- Team membership and roles
- Team involvement on both the whole-class level and the individual student level
- Data-based problem solving (see the RtI Implementation Guidelines for Problem Solving at the end of chapter 4)
- Data-based decision points within the tiers (see the RtI Decision-Making Guide at the end of this chapter)
- Establishment of a communication system that includes notification and involvement of parents
- Documentation forms and procedures

Documentation forms should cover communication with parents, teacher interviews, parent interviews, the team process itself, definition of outcome goals, observations of the student, strategies and instruction levels to be used, identified interventionists/teachers, fidelity of implementation, and progress monitoring.

Lessons Learned: The guidelines do not have to be overwhelming. Keep the district RtI manual simple, and all information should be transparent. Focus on describing resources, assessments, and decision points that serve as a framework for analyzing data for the student's intervention level. Include a reference guide to the instructional strategies to be used and the tools for measuring progress available to teachers within your framework (see figure 2.2).

Selecting the Campus Team

An essential component in sustaining RtI campus problem solving is understanding the campus RtI team process and identifying the most suitable team members. It is crucial that campus administrators objectively evaluate the effectiveness of current team members and meeting procedures. The administrator's awareness of the resistance to change and potential barriers to successful RtI is vital for the appropriate selection of staff members.

The roles of the campus team members are to increase support for high-quality curriculum and instruction through collaboration and problem solving with staff, administrators, and parents based on data collected; to provide systematic support to teachers; to assist in aligning existing school resources for support of students and teachers; and to focus the decision-making process on data analysis. The most effective teams have a wide variety of expertise and experience across multiple areas. Core team members are supplemented by invited members as needed (table 2.1).

Table 2.1. Members of the campus RtI team

Core Members	Invited Members (as Needed)
1. Campus principal (preferred) or a designee who has decision-making authority regarding curriculum, supports, and budget issues 2. The referring teacher 3. At least one general education teacher familiar with the curriculum 4. Intervention specialist 5. Staff member knowledgeable about assessment and documentation 6. Parent of child	1. School psychologist 2. Reading/literacy specialist 3. Math specialist 4. District-level interventionists 5. Speech therapist 6. Occupational therapist 7. Counselor for struggling learners 8. Campus counselor 9. School nurse 10. Special education support/inclusion teacher

The campus RtI team engages in two distinct functions. One is to analyze the universal screening data in order to interpret trends and identify struggling learners who fall below the predetermined cutoff score. The team reviews the data to determine whether there are deficits in Tier 1 curriculum or delivery of instruction that may be contributing to students' inability to meet standards. The team uses the data in this sense to provide consultation to teachers and other staff on improving Tier 1 interventions and whole-class instruction. The second function of the team is student-centered, focusing on individual student needs. The team carries out this function after Tier 1 problem solving has been addressed and fidelity of curriculum and instruction is established. At this time, the team problem-solves to decide on individual interventions aimed at increasing the learning rate of the struggling learner.

Having staff members who are skilled in the areas of assessment and interventions is necessary, of course, but the selected team members absolutely must be motivated to participate in the RtI process. If a staff member is skilled but is not motivated or is not supportive of RtI, *do not* select this person for the team. (Such individuals are simply not ready yet, and that is okay. With time and training, they will be.) Even though a staff member may be skilled, an unsupportive attitude will poison the problem-solving process, as barriers will constantly weigh down team growth and effectiveness. On the other hand, a highly motivated staff member who has a strong positive attitude toward RtI but demonstrates skill deficits may be a very good person to select for the team, because staff development can provide the needed skills. This staff member may become an effective leader and promoter of the process, and public relations is an extremely valuable asset in the development of RtI. Other traits to look for in team members are that they are viewed as approachable and are respected by the campus staff. Team membership should be regarded as a privilege and not as "just another committee I am assigned to."

Lessons Learned: One campus administrator decided to ask a resistant team member to join the RtI team because she was a highly respected veteran teacher. The administrator was well aware this teacher had publicly stated opposition to the RtI process and on more than one occasion had said that she was near retirement and would be "long gone" before RtI was functional on the campus. The administrator thought that the staff development afforded to team members would change the teacher's attitude. What the administrator did not count on was that the teacher was not at all motivated to accept the change. Within the first six months of team development, the teacher became so disruptive to the process (by not collaboratively participating) that she was asked to leave the team. This caused problems with staff morale because the team was then perceived and promoted (by guess who) as an elitist group, which was not true. Typically, campus teachers will develop trust and respect for the team during the first year of RtI implementation, but because of the damage caused by this initial team selection, the RtI team on that campus needed two full years to gain acceptance and respect.

Organizing the Campus Team

When preparing to establish the campus RtI team, the campus principal must attend to details such as finding space for team meetings and file storage, purchasing supplies, and assigning a responsible person to help with duplication of forms. The principal should train all office staff on handling requests for campus RtI team assistance. The principal must also inventory resources available on the campus within classrooms (textbooks, technology, etc.), as well as school-wide resources, such as volunteers, peer tutoring, and availability of school psychologists, speech and language pathologists, social workers, physical therapists, and paraeducators. Additionally, any district-level supports that may be available, particularly with regard to staff development, should be evaluated. Finally, the principal must inventory resources available from the parents and within the community at large (such as after-school programs, support groups, community social programs, and tutoring). Parents are an important resource for schools because they know their children and their difficulties very well. Parents are vital in helping the team develop interventions.

paraeducators Support members of the learning and teaching team who ensure that students receive multiple levels of support in schools.

Once the team members have been selected and have received the initial RtI training, it is important for the principal to schedule weekly meeting times that are sacred (cannot be changed). The principal should publish these dates and distribute the schedule to staff and parents.

Now it is time to define the roles of the team members. The campus administrator is usually the chair of the team. Other roles can be standing for particular members, or they can be rotated per student case. Among the many ways to clarify specific roles, the following are the most common:

Chairperson: In most instances, the campus administrator chairs the team. The chairperson is primarily responsible for running the team's meetings and following a meeting agenda. The chair is responsible for the entire meeting process, including making sure that parents have been contacted and informed, but may choose to appoint a team member to be in charge of sending out notices and preparing the team for the meeting. During the meeting itself, the chairperson welcomes all in attendance, reviews the purpose of the meeting, and sets goals for the meeting. Next, the chair presents the concerns in terms of the data collected, guides the team in the problem-solving process, and supports the team in developing academic and behavioral strategies and the final intervention plan. Finally, the chairperson closes the meeting with a summary of the meeting discussion and agreed-upon plan and sets a time for the team to reconvene to discuss student progress. Outside of meetings, the chair responds to those who wish to refer a student and supplies them with preliminary information about the documentation the team will need. Additionally, the chairperson checks with the case manager on a regular basis to ensure that all processes are being followed with fidelity.

Timekeeper: The person in this position helps all members stay focused, by using timing techniques and bringing staff back to topic when discussions stray. The timekeeper holds the team to its schedule within meetings and gives updates on progress within the time limits as needed.

Case manager: This person is someone who can consult and collaborate with all staff to ensure fidelity of assessments and interventions. The case manager meets with the referring teacher to determine if resource allocation is sufficient, necessary materials are available, and support personnel for interventions are showing up at designated times. The case manager has a responsibility to the student, the parents, and the RtI team for ensuring that the process is going as planned, including helping the teacher of record and the designated interventionist make sure that all documentation forms are completed in a timely manner.

Document facilitator: This person is mainly responsible for documenting all aspects of the RtI team process, beginning at Tier 2. The document facilitator helps the referring teacher collate previous Tier 1 data and becomes primarily responsible for the processes of data collection and documentation that begin in Tier 2. This person might not be the one to carry out the assessments but is the one who ensures that they are documented correctly. This facilitator is also responsible for taking meeting minutes and notes, filling out required forms, and organizing all RtI team documents.

Critical to problem solving are the forms used to document the fidelity of the RtI process. The following is an example of the flow of data collection:

Universal screening results and documentation
- Classroom observations
- Review of records
- Documentation of level of curriculum taught and instructional intervention
- Parent notification of concerns

RtI invitation to participate

- Parent notification of RtI meeting
- Teacher/staff notification of RtI meeting
- Problem identification using multiple data sources
- Documentation of classroom observations
- Documentation of problem-solving meeting
- Intervention plan
- Results of progress monitoring/curriculum-based measurements (CBM)
- Progress reports

Documentation of progress monitoring/CBM results

- Description of interventions
- Student work samples
- Follow-up documentation of fidelity
- Data for formal request for multidisciplinary assessment: health history, progress reports, and campus RtI team reports (minutes and notes)

Remember that the campus team's chairperson is responsible for checking with team case managers to make sure all forms are completed at the specified time in the process.

curriculum-based measurement (CBM) Any set of assessment procedures that use direct observation and recording of a student's performance in a local curriculum to gather information for making instructional decisions.

RtI/MTSS Plan for District Implementation

Rationale: RtI/MTSS guides data-driven decisions about student needs and progress, allowing educators to teach effectively, to design prescriptive academic and social-emotional interventions, and to challenge and inspire students. A well-defined MTSS system is also necessary to comply with federal and state laws and statutes.

Goal: To develop, implement, and support a framework for effective RtI/MTSS practices that are horizontally and vertically aligned and that result in student growth.

Objectives: Process development, professional development, coaching, and student progress.

Process Development	Professional Development and Coaching	Student Progress
Develop a blueprint of level-specific leadership, intervention, and campus processes available to MTSS teams	*Provide initial and ongoing MTSS PD and coaching for all levels of leadership and staff*	*Maintain integrity of student progress by using data-based decisions and student response (progress monitoring) to determine efficacy of decision making*
Indicators:	**Indicators:**	**Indicators:**
<ul><li>A process is in place for research-based instruction and interventions with appropriate documentation.</li><li>Campus committees/teams are represented by members within layers of leadership and skill/content areas.</li><li>Campus committees/teams continuously evaluate the needs of the staff and students and adjust within an MTSS blueprint as necessary to ensure student and teacher success.</li><li>MTSS resources and documents will be uniformly developed and utilized within a streamlined data management system used by the district.</li></ul>	<ul><li>Ongoing MTSS PD is readily available and tailored to the needs of each campus through consultation and coaching.</li><li>Real-time support is available to teachers and campuses as they work toward integrity of framework.</li><li>A tiered e-course training model has been designed.</li><li>An integrated PD plan connects curriculum, instruction, and emotional/behavioral practices within NISD.</li></ul>	<ul><li>MTSS data are easily accessible and electronically maintained.</li><li>Documentation is easily accessible, streamlined, and maintained electronically.</li><li>All teachers use data to monitor student growth weekly with relative ease.</li><li>Student data and documentation transitions with students when they move to a new campus.</li><li>District- and campus-level staff can assess the effectiveness of instruction and interventions and adjust curriculum, instruction, and emotional supports with ease.</li></ul>
Essential Questions:	**Essential Questions:**	**Essential Questions:**
<ul><li>Is the framework well structured to allow for consistency of implementation?</li><li>Is the framework flexible to meet unique campus needs?</li><li>Are there avenues to explore when integrity of problem solving is compromised?</li></ul>	<ul><li>Does the training represent both a top-down and bottom-up effort?</li><li>Does the training represent MTSS and an "all education" initiative and not just another "add on" process?</li></ul>	<ul><li>Does existing technology structure allow for secure housing and simple access/transfer of student MTSS data?</li><li>What barriers exist that slow the process of data aggregation and documentation?</li><li>How can these barriers be addressed?</li></ul>

RtI Decision-Making Guide

TIER 1
Universal screening: fall, spring, winter

1. Cut-off score = 25th percentile.
2. Principal chairs a meeting with RtI team. Data analysis to identify trends in students falling below cutoff score. Consultation with teachers occurs regarding curriculum and instructional practices.
3. Teachers implement core curriculum and strategies for 6–8 weeks. Review classroom data and analyze progress of struggling learners with CBMs or classroom-based assessments.

   * *Decision point:* Identify students who continue to fall below cutoff score and demonstrate a lack of progress, falling within the bottom 10 percent of students based on district norms. Schedule RtI meeting to discuss their move to Tier 2.

TIER 2
Strategic interventions: 9–12 weeks; repeat

1. Use researched fluency learning rates (Fuchs, Deno, Shapiro, AIMSweb, etc.).
   * Establish baseline scores and develop aimline (goal).
   * Determine number of weeks of intervention, a 30-minute session 2 or 3 days per week.
   * Problem-solve intervention (standard protocol).
   * Assign case manager, assessment support, and intervention support.
   * Begin intervention.
   * Progress monitoring 2 times per week.

     * *Decision point:* Weeks 4–6. Use a 3- or 4-data-point decision rule to monitor progress, and problem-solve if intervention needs to be altered.

   * Continue intervention.

     * *Decision point:* Weeks 9–12. Reconvene RtI team, and analyze data. If learning rate improves according to aimline, continue intervention. If not, change intervention and monitor for a repeat of weeks 9–12 ; *or* if learning rate continues to fall significantly below that of peers (10th percentile), refer student to Tier 3.

TIER 3
Intensive interventions

1. Increase intensity of intervention to two 30-minute sessions per day, 5 days a week, conducted by trained support personnel. RtI team may also add to standard protocol interventions.
2. Increase progress monitoring to 3 times per week.

   * *Decision point*: Weeks 9–12. If learning rate increases, continue intervention. If learning rate does not increase or if intensity of intervention is judged to be long-term based upon resources, refer student for a comprehensive evaluation.

   * *Decision point:* IEP (individualized education plan) team convenes to review comprehensive evaluation and determine special education eligibility. If student is deemed eligible, IEPs are developed based on all data. Progress monitoring continues. Student receives Tier 1 and Tier 3 interventions.

Chapter 3

Tier 1

*Supporting All Students through
Universal Screening and Interventions*

Response to Intervention is a general education process that is designed to support struggling learners both academically and behaviorally. Each of the three tiers in the RtI model represents particular methods of assessment, instructional strategies, and increased targeted instructional interventions. The interventions are unique to the needs of the individual student as determined through campus team collaboration and conversations (see figures 1.1–1.3).

Currently, most school districts have an identified RtI process in place. The issue is that many of these processes have drifted from their original intent. Organizational drift occurs when personnel change, resources are underfunded or underutilized, and ongoing professional development halts.

Tier 1 is the foundation of the RtI process. Its purpose is simply to provide good teaching strategies and support for all students. This tier is best described as implementing core grade-level curriculum and positive behavior strategies that should effectively meet the needs of the majority of the students enrolled. (The baseline expectation is that 80 percent of student success will occur within Tier 1.) The differentiated instruction and strategies implemented at this stage are meant to be preventive and proactive (identify problems, intervene with sound curriculum and instruction, and use research-based strategies to promote learning). Therefore, instructional variables (such as delivery of instruction by using graphic organizers or computer-assisted instruction), curricular variables (such as entry point into the curriculum skill level or choice of a particular skill to work on), school organization (such as grouping teachers into teams according to grade level or content area), and structural variables (such as class schedules and space available for additional instruction and intervention) are examined and modified to increase the probability of success within the general education classroom.

preventive Refers to action (such as early intervention) undertaken to avoid failure.

proactive Refers to action that anticipates future needs or problems, such as putting supports in place to increase the probability of successful learning outcomes and positive behaviors in the classroom.

instructional variable A quantifiable event or circumstance related to the action, practice, or profession of teaching.

curricular variable A quantifiable event or circumstance related to the instruction of students in the schools.

structural variables Quantifiable events or circumstances related to a school system's pattern of organization.

The philosophy guiding Tier 1 problem solving and analysis is to ensure student success within the general education environment by providing proactive instruction (research-based), effective teaching strategies that focus on individual learning styles, and supports for positive behavior. Underlying the philosophy is the knowledge that prevention and early intervention are more time- and cost-efficient and more likely to succeed than remediation strategies, which typically occur after a problem is already established and has been identified.

Universal Screening for Academic and Behavioral Skills

As in all RtI tiers, assessment guides the Tier 1 data analysis and decision making. The first and most important step in the data conversation, called universal screening (or school-wide screening), occurs in Tier 1. This assessment is designed to evaluate overall student academic and behavioral progress and also to identify students whose performance is not consistent with that of their peers. The fundamental questions at this stage of RtI are:

1. All else being equal, are more than 20 percent of the students falling below expected levels in both reading and math?
2. Do the data show trends by content or grade level (for instance, are large numbers of students not meeting expectations)?
3. Once trends are analyzed, are there students who continue to struggle and are not already identified as tiered students, special education students, or Section 504 students (e.g., dyslexia)?

The ultimate goal of universal screening is to develop research-based instructional practices that minimize failure and maximize success for all students within their grade-level general education curriculum and expectations.

Universal screening begins early in the school year (in the fall), is given to all students, and is administered one or two additional times during the year (winter and spring). A good screening process will quickly identify grade- and campus-level trends in reading and math, as well as students who are candidates for additional instructional intervention. The screening will also help identify subgroups of students on the campus or within the district who show the most and least student progress. This in turn will lead to identifying support that may be necessary for some teachers and student subgroups (such as bilingual or English language learners).

Universal screening can be curriculum-based measurements (CBMs, discussed in Chapter 4), district benchmark assessments, state-mandated tests, and other types of assessment that the district has identified as useful. Typically the fall data are collected in September, the winter data in January, and the spring data in April/May. The district should establish guidelines for cutoff scores that will guide decision making for interventions. (Note: It is recommended that the cutoff scores be established by district-level curriculum coordinators/specialists to ensure consistency across the district when making decisions at Tier 1. See "Data for Identifying Struggling Learners," on page 39, for a discussion of cutoff scores.)

It is important that the district-level RtI team establish the dates for universal screening and place them on the testing calendar. In addition, campus administrators must convey to their staff the necessity of both completing the universal screening on all students and documenting the results within the time designated. In my experience, the fidelity of the administration and reporting of the universal screening has varied on many campuses that were implementing this form of assessment. Teachers must understand that Tier 1 decision making cannot begin unless the data are complete, so all teachers must submit their full results at the required time.

Lessons Learned: The traditional universal screener will not have a one-to-one correspondence to grade-level state standards. Rather, it assesses essential grade-level foundational skill fluency, based on national/state norms. This type of data allows for analysis of grade-level student strengths and weaknesses, which is needed for trend analysis of Tier 1 instructional practices. The measures are basic reading skill fluency, reading comprehension fluency, math computational fluency, and applied problem fluency. Teachers often mistake this analysis for a measurement of growth toward a mastery criterion found on state assessments. That confusion leads teachers to misunderstand the value of the data. Students who perform above the cutoff score on this measure demonstrate an automaticity with foundational skills necessary for learning within the grade-level curriculum; therefore, they are best served with strong Tier 1 instructional practices and supports. Those who do not may need additional instruction and learning strategies offered within a Tier 2 or Tier 3 situation. These data also offer great opportunities for campus-based professional learning communities to problem solve around identified trends. Several schools I have worked with have found reading instructional weaknesses within trends for certain grade levels and were able to adopt additional curriculum supports to close the gaps for the many learners needing additional tutoring at grade level.

School districts are currently conducting universal screenings. Many, however, are either using incorrect assessment instruments or not analyzing the results correctly. The measure should be norm referenced, not criterion referenced. It should sample the critical skills necessary for student success at each grade level.

The instrument should also provide national or state norms to use as comparisons. It is vitally important for the school district to use caution when selecting the screening tool as well as providing staff members with professional development in how to understand and analyze the data.

Lessons Learned: Because universal screenings are conducted 3 times per year, it is critical that they be brief. Often schools use longer assessments that are diagnostic and take time away from student instructional time. A very good universal screener is brief and easy to administer, and the results are easy to disaggregate and understand. Good examples of universal screeners that meet these criteria are AimsWeb, DIBELS, Easy CBM, and CBMs found on the website Intervention Central (interventioncentral. org). Although diagnostic data are important and often requested by teachers, such data are not used in universal screening. Diagnostic data come into play once the universal screening is completed and potential Tier 2 students are identified.

At Tier 1, the RtI campus team is responsible for fostering communication with grade-level professional learning communities and aiding individual teachers in the proper analysis and use of screening data. Although screening data may not be as robust for identifying individual student problems as more-intensive diagnostic assessments are, they yield valuable information about core curricular and behavioral expectations within the school system. The information serves three purposes (Batsche et al. 2005):

- Provides information useful for evaluating class performance and identifying needed teacher supports
- Identifies students who need further evaluation and increased intensity of intervention (Tier 2)
- Identifies students who may slip through the cracks at one level of assessment but be caught by another

What should be measured at the universal screening level?

- Effectiveness of core curriculum
- Required developmental and prerequisite skills
- Student background information
- Skills that are the building blocks for acquiring higher-order skills

When deciding which core curriculum variables to include in the screening, it is important to enlist district specialists in reading, writing, and math. Besides helping to identify the skills to be screened, these specialists can inform the district-level RtI committee on state mandates and recommendations regarding assessment and intervention and how they are currently being implemented in the district. For example, the National Reading Panel for the Elementary and Secondary Education Act (ESEA) identified the essential components of reading instruction as phonemic awareness, phonics, vocabulary development, reading fluency, oral reading skills, and reading comprehension skills. The reading specialists can review the current district-wide assessments and recommend changes to ensure that they measure these components. Data collected should then be linked with instructional outcomes at each grade level, based on reading skill acquisition.

In order to sustain a robust RtI problem-solving process, a district needs to develop frameworks in which campus teams use data to solve problems in a consistent and proactive manner. Districts that do not provide this guidance often drift from the intent of the prevention and intervention process and find it very difficult to have consistency across campuses. The inconsistency causes confusion among parents about how their children are being supported when they demonstrate difficulty learning new concepts, and it fuels staff dissatisfaction with supports and services in place to promote student growth. Inconsistency can also severely limit the effectiveness of professional development opportunities. A strong framework for the analysis of universal screening data promotes conversations that are viewed as supportive of grade-level curricular resources; such resources must be in place to enhance the growth of all students on the campus. The universal screening data allow for open and honest discussions on whether the curriculum and teaching strategies used in the classroom are research-based and are being consistently implemented as they were intended to be (that is, with fidelity). Quite often campus staff will make statements such as "We are already doing that," when in reality the strategies being used are frequently not delivered in the manner in which they were designed.

phonemic awareness Awareness of the sounds of language and how they make up words and sentences.

phonics An instructional design that involves teaching children to read by connecting sounds with letters or groups of letters.

Lessons Learned: If an administrator is not actively involved in the problem-solving process, it will be difficult for campus RtI teams to have conversations surrounding trends that find weaknesses in instructional practices. It is imperative that campus leaders are visible and provide positive encouragement to promote the changes necessary to address areas of concern. Campuses that successfully develop goals using teacher-based strategies and district-supplied resources will have the strongest results in promoting student growth. If trend analysis and the adopted changes are to be intentional and viable, the campus administrator must also structure resources and professional development into the campus planning process. The best way to address trends is to provide professional learning community opportunities that allow teachers to be active participants in the problem solutions.

Instruments for Assessing Academic Skills

The best place to begin when choosing the screening assessment is to analyze the district-wide assessments that are currently in place. Typically states have mandated or recommended assessments in the early elementary grades for reading, math, and writing. Analyze the data derived from those assessments, and then add or subtract assessments as your curriculum specialists recommend.

The most important aspect of this analysis is that the district adopts assessments for all students that are consistent across all grade levels. Some states focus intensive interventions and assessments in reading for kindergarten through third grade because of the Reading First initiative outlined in the No Child Left Behind Act (now known as ESSA). These tools need to be analyzed to determine how they can be extended to the higher grades. Also, these tools are often diagnostic in nature but have the features that are essential for a good screener as well. If so, identify which portions of the assessments are suitable for use as a universal screener and adopt them as the screener for all students 3 times a year. If a suitable screener is not available within the assessment tool, adopt one that is brief (2 to 5 minutes), easy to administer, and easy to score that can be used 3 times per year for all students.

When choosing universal screening instruments, it is important to follow some simple guidelines:

- The assessment instrument ensures the validity of the information collected. (That is, it screens for particular skills to identify students who may be in danger of failing the subject area.)
- The assessment is research-based, per ESSA and state standards.
- The assessment is easy to administer.
- Teachers know how to administer the assessment and interpret the data. (If not, develop training sessions for the teachers.)
- The data are presented in an easy-to-follow format for decision making.

Reading First initiative A process whereby states and districts receive support from the federal government for applying scientifically based research to ensure that all children learn to read well by the end of third grade.

developmental skill progression The process of acquiring the basic skills necessary for learning to occur.

validity The degree to which a test measures what it was designed to measure.

Lessons Learned: Districts that have strong, sustainable RtI systems are ones that proactively analyze their assessment practices yearly for collecting Tier 1 curriculum benchmark data (summative data that are criterion-referenced and often aligned to state testing standards). Once the district analyzes the utility of the practices, it then selects and adds curriculum-based measurements and additional grade-level criterion- or norm-referenced tests to the universal screening lists. Instruments that have been analyzed and adopted across many districts nationwide include, but are not limited to, the following:

Curriculum-based measurements (reading, math, writing)

- AIMSweb
- CBM Warehouse (reading and math CBM probe development)
- Dynamic Indicators of Basic Early Literacy Skills (DIBELS) 6th Edition
- DIBELS Next
- IDEL (Spanish DIBELS)
- easyCBM
- Istation
- Measures of Academic Progress (MAP)
- Monitoring Basic Skills Progress (MBSP)
- STAR 360, Renaissance Reading and Math
- System to Enhance Educational Performance (STEEP)
- RAPS 360
- Texas Primary Reading Inventory (TPRI)

norm-referenced assessment A measure of performance in terms of an individual's standing in some known group, such as all of a district's students at a particular grade level.

criterion-referenced assessment A measure of performance in terms of a clearly defined learning task.

Data for Identifying Struggling Learners

A district's universal screening plan can be developed to compare a student's performance with local norms, state norms, or national norms, based on grade level. If the district would like to use local norms, its screening system will need to gather all student scores for the grade level and then arrange the data by percentile ranks. District specialists within each curricular area help identify which scores fall within the percentile that indicates struggling learners. This percentile then becomes the cutoff score used to identify struggling learners. If the district prefers, it can choose to use state or national scores that are norm-referenced and often are reported as percentile or quartile scores. These scores represent a national sample of student performance that can be compared with district screening data to determine the cutoff score.

cutoff score Within RtI, a preset score set to help identify struggling learners during universal screening at Tier 1. The most common cutoff score used by school districts is set at the 25th percentile based on local, state, or national norms.

The widely accepted and researched cutoff score falls at the 25th percentile and is designed to identify the bottom 15 to 20 percent of students at grade level.

When analyzing universal screening data, administrators and the RtI team typically begin by looking for patterns within the classroom, grade level, campus, or district, where data suggest that more than 20 percent of the student population is falling below the cutoff score. The presiding philosophy at this stage is that if more than 20 percent of the students in the universal screening fall below the cutoff score, the reason is not a within-student issue. Instead, it may indicate that Tier 1 foundations of core curriculum and instruction need to be altered to meet the needs of the students. The data should be analyzed to determine whether the concerns are district-wide, school-wide, grade-level, or classroom-based. Be careful here. This step is extremely important. All students should be judged against the same cutoff scores. Certain student populations—such as those with English as a second language, low-income students, and so on—should not be assigned a higher percentage rate of failure to meet cutoff standards. If the data show such a pattern, then the emphasis of RtI should be on redesigning the curriculum and instruction to meet the needs of the population.

within-student issue An issue that is due to a student's learning and emotional/behavioral strengths and weaknesses.

phoneme segmentation The ability to break up and identify the sounds within words.

sound blending The blending of sounds together to form words.

fluency An acceptable level of mastery of a skill.

Lessons Learned: One campus RtI team found that 35 percent of its students with English as a second language performed below the identified cutoff score for first-grade expectations in reading. The data also revealed that the students were primarily showing deficits in the areas of phoneme segmentation, sound blending, and fluency. The RtI team then invited district- and campus-level reading specialists and a bilingual specialist to a meeting to evaluate the curriculum. The team examined instructional strands on the identified areas with respect to expected language learning rates, skill introduction, repeated drills, and supplemental teaching strategies and was able to pinpoint weaknesses in the instructional design. This resulted in designing staff training for understanding language as it relates to the development of reading skills, and adding research-based curriculum materials and bilingual teaching strategies for the general education teachers to use as Tier 1 supports for students. In the next review of universal screening data, the RtI team noted an upward trend in learning rates for the identified students, indicating that the added support in Tier 1 was having a positive effect.

Another example of using universal screening data to enhance Tier 1 supports happened at a campus where the demographics of the student population included low socioeconomic variables (poverty). The initial universal screening showed a large portion of the kindergarten and first-grade students falling below the designated cutoff scores in reading (approximately

38 percent). The RtI team analyzed the data and determined that many of the students might not have had a strong language experience to draw on for language and reading development. The campus principal asked for support from the district speech pathologist, who immediately consulted with the kindergarten and first-grade teams. Together they developed lesson plans with increased language enrichment activities. The speech pathologist also went into the classrooms and modeled whole-class instructional strategies for the teachers to use to increase the language experience of the students. The RtI team noticed a significant increase in reading skills for the kindergarten and first-grade students upon reviewing the next set of universal screening data.

After analyzing the data, the RtI team either rules out curriculum and teaching practices as causes of concern or else takes action to improve them where needed. Once that has been done, the RtI team can focus on the 15 to 20 percent of students who remain below the cutoff score. These students are then designated as struggling learners, and the classroom teacher will be given training and support to boost their learning within the Tier 1 instructional practices.

The best way to determine factors affecting student learning is to spend additional time within the RtI meeting reviewing data on those students falling below the universal screening cutoff score; this requires an analysis of multiple data sources. The review should determine what additional diagnostic assessments are needed for decision making and goal setting within the RtI problem-solving process. Diagnostic assessments provide extensive and important information about individual student learning, which makes them the best assessments to use to understand the greatest needs of the identified student. Because diagnostic measures are time-intensive and expensive, they are typically administered only to the students identified for additional instruction and intervention. Diagnostic assessments will help the RtI campus team determine what skills are deficient, and they are needed for selection of appropriate instructional strategies and interventions. Often school districts will purchase assessment systems that include the universal screeners as well as the additional diagnostic assessments.

Meanwhile, student progress should be monitored to determine if a higher level of intervention is needed (Tier 2). Once a child is identified as a struggling learner at Tier 1, monitoring of student growth is essential. Monitoring should also include consistency in the delivery of instruction, documentation of the various strategies being used, instructional differentiation practices, small group placements, and rates of learning for 4 to 6 weeks. "Fidelity of instruction" simply means that the teachers are consistently carrying out the core curriculum and instructional strategies as they were designed. The RtI team should moni-

documentation Any material (such as student products, tests, written reports) containing data gathered during the RtI process.

tor both teacher support and student progress once a week to see whether the student makes progress as the teacher implements strategies. The team needs to ascertain if the student acquires the necessary skills identified as deficient for grade-level success by the additional teacher support given. If the student does not show the progress expected by the RtI team within the designated time recommended in a district-wide framework, then the RtI committee should schedule a meeting and notify the teacher and student's parents of the meeting. At the meeting, it is essential that all of the documentation of additional teaching strategies and differentiated instructional interventions be thoroughly reviewed. This discussion should also consider any behavioral issues that may be affecting learning, such as attention span, anxiety, trauma, or stress. Once the analysis is complete, the team may recommend additional Tier 1 instructional strategies or interventions, or add on Tier 2 supports.

Diagnostic assessments (reading, math, writing)

- DIBELS 6th Edition
- DIBELS Next
- IDEL (Spanish DIBELS)
- Istation
- Measures of Academic Progress (MAP)
- STAR 360, Renaissance Reading and Math
- RAPS 360
- Texas Primary Reading Inventory (TPRI)

Lessons Learned: When universal screening data are available, it is common for teachers to look first for students who are falling below the cutoff score and immediately try to move them to a Tier 2 intervention. That approach can send everyone down the wrong path. It is very important that the team use a drill-down process to avoid the possibility of designing a flawed instructional intervention. The drill-down process should begin when the team meets (3 times per year) to analyze the trend in the data. The process must differentiate the issues that need to be corrected through Tier 1 instruction (i.e., the trend indicates that instructional issues are the reason too many students do not have the necessary skills) from issues within the individual student (academic or emotional/behavioral). Once the data are analyzed for trends, the next step is to review data on students who fall below the cutoff score. If the students have been identified and are already receiving interventions, the team should look to see if they are demonstrating growth and forward the information to the appropriate special education department point person on the campus or Section 504 department point person. In the final phase of the drill-down process, the RtI team analyzes multiple data sources on individual students remaining on the list. Once this is accomplished, the team then schedules a meeting to include the teacher(s) working with the student and assigns any additional diagnostic assessment that will aid in the decision to move to a Tier 2 level of intervention. (See Appendix D, Multiple Sources of Data.)

Evaluation of Behavioral Skills and Supports

In addition to academic skills, Tier 1 assessment includes behavioral screening. This is an area that is lacking in many school districts. It is important that the district recommend a framework for supporting student emotional and behavioral needs. This framework should be developed with district-level administrators who support guidance counselors and behavior specialists. Suggested screening measures include reviewing the following school records:

- Attendance
- Tardies
- Office referrals (note time of day, referring teacher, and setting where the behavior occurred)
- Disciplinary actions taken (parent call, detention, suspension)
- District-adopted behavior screening instrument

Tier 1 data must include observations of classroom and other situations that note whether positive behavioral supports are in place, such as the following examples:

- Class rules are posted and visible.
- Positive and negative consequences are clear, immediately given, linked to behaviors, and consistently implemented.
- Social skills and character programs are introduced, modeled, and reinforced.
- Organization of learning areas (physical space designated for learning) is evident.
- Routines and schedules are clear.
- Study/learning strategies and teacher's expectations of students are taught.
- Active supervision and monitoring of students are evident.
- Discipline is enforced in a firm and fair manner.

Along with such observations, the district may also choose to purchase a student risk screening instrument that would be used with all students, such as one of these:

- BASC-2 Behavioral and Emotional Screening System (BASC-2 BESS)
- Social, Academic, and Emotional Behavior Risk Screener (SAEBRS)
- Student Risk Screening Scale (SRSS)

The assessment of behavior at Tier 1 is designed to focus on prevention and early intervention, using classroom and school-wide positive behavior and social emotional supports. It is much easier to support changes in behavior at this level. Behavioral interventions have a much higher rate of success when they are addressed early, positively, and proactively at Tier 1.

Universal Academic Interventions

The RtI problem-solving process requires that the design of the Tier 1 instructional strategies, supports, and differentiated interventions focus on how students are affected by a variety of instructional variables at their grade level:

- The nature of the instruction (resources, materials, curriculum, and programs used within lecture and small group situations)
- The time allocated to the delivery of instruction (including guided practice of introduced skills)
- Prerequisite skills students have mastered prior to delivery of instruction
- The validity of the instructional practices
- The fidelity of the implementation of instructional strategies or programs

It is paramount that staff understand that the purpose of this approach is not to generate a referral to determine student eligibility for special programs or services. Rather, the focus is on *designing and implementing effective instructional practices*. As mentioned earlier, the goal of universal screening is to develop research-based instructional practices that minimize failure and maximize success for all students. The greater the needs of the learner, the greater the demand on instructional design and implementation. The core academic program needs to be evaluated to determine whether the instruction provided on the essential elements is designed to meet the needs of most of the students. Once the academic program has been shown to be meeting those needs, additional instructional strategies will focus on the particular needs of some of the students. (Remember, one size does not fit all.) At this level of intervention, the focus is on targeting essential grade-level skills, supporting differentiated instructional practices, monitoring student responses, and training teachers in critical skills.

Tier 1 instruction focuses on all learners by using instructional practices geared to assessment, research-based student learning strategies, and skills development for both students and teachers. By receiving training, teachers and staff become skilled in planning and implementing research-based instructional practices that include curriculum, delivery of instruction, and positive behavior support systems.

Tier 1 instructional strategies and support should focus on all student learning. It is important for staff to understand that instructional intervention is not a program to enhance learning at Tier 1—it is *effective core instruction*. According to Hattie (2009, p. 22), "visible teaching and learning" by teachers and students is what makes the most significant impact on student growth. He defines visible teaching and learning as occurring when "learning is the explicit goal, when it is appropriately challenging, when the teacher and student both seek to ascertain whether and to what degree the challenging goal is attained, and when there is deliberate practice aimed at attaining mastery of the goal, when there is feedback given and sought, and when there are active, passionate, and engaging people (teacher, student, peers, and so on) participating in the act of learning."

That statement sums up the overall goal of Tier 1 discussions within an RtI framework. The instructional strategies and interventions discussed should follow this framework for producing the maximum student growth within the classroom setting. The team should analyze innovative practices being implemented and the consequences of those practices (positive and negative) for all students. It is essential that the team discuss all variables surrounding teaching practices within the grade level or content area to provide optimal supports for strengthening instructional practices. Ultimately, a strong foundation within Tier 1 instruction is imperative to all involved; without that foundation, it will be very difficult to affect individual student growth when adding or layering on additional individualized instruction in Tier 2 or 3.

To promote sustainability of a strong RtI problem-solving process, it is crucial that the campus teams embrace the continued use of research-based instructional practices. Several publications and supports related to research-based curriculum, strategies, and training are available and are referenced in Appendix C (Online Resources).

There has been much confusion and anxiety regarding where to find good research-based strategies for Tier 1 supports. The best way to accomplish this is for the curriculum specialists in the school district to identify needs based on data. Once the curriculum specialists identify campus needs, the appropriate strategies can be referenced in the district framework for suggested Tier 1 strategies and supports. Often teachers want a checklist of strategies or a binder of programs to guide them through Tier 1, but it is critical that all staff and parents understand that Tier 1 supports are focused on good instructional design and delivery and not on a particular program. Therefore, it is not recommended that teachers be given a checklist or binder of particular programs; instead, the campus team should guide teachers to the research-based practices listed in the district framework through effective consultation and staff development.

An important aspect of instruction is the differentiation of delivery of the content, process, and product to ensure that all learners improve their levels of achievement. It is no mystery that maximizing instructional time highly correlates with increased learning. When implementing Tier 1, teachers should feel supported in their efforts to optimize their time in the classroom so that they can accomplish the following:

differentiated instruction An approach to teaching and learning in which students have multiple options for taking in information and making sense of ideas; requires teachers to be flexible in adjusting their methods and the curriculum to suit students, rather than expecting students to modify themselves for the curriculum.

- Increase opportunities to respond within the context of the lesson.
- Increase opportunities to build on prior knowledge and enhance success within the content being discussed.
- Alter the instruction delivery so that the pace is appropriate.
- Differentiate the instruction to increase the opportunity for all learners to understand.

Therefore, Tier 1 instruction is focused on scheduling of instruction, student grouping (small groups, guided learning in reading and math, cooperative learning opportunities), and delivery of instruction. This can be done with continuous monitoring of grade-level progress as well as weekly analyses by the professional learning community of instructional practices within the grade-level core curriculum.

Teachers will need a variety of supports for implementing strongly differentiated Tier 1 instructional practices in their classrooms. Essential to increasing student achievement is the notion that the core curriculum is research-based and delivered consistently on a daily basis. In addition to receiving training, teachers must be given the time to deliver the needed instruction to their students. To achieve this, the administration staff, teaching staff, and consulting specialists must coordinate their efforts. Along with the grade-level curriculum, teachers will be presenting optimal opportunities to students with a variety of needs in Tier 1. To gain the knowledge and resources required to do so, teachers must have access to consultants in relevant areas of specialization (for example, dyslexia, bilingual, behavior, and so on).

When supporting struggling learners in Tier 1, teachers will need information about the skills students need for progressing in the curriculum, particularly in reading and math. Reading is easier to address because state and federal initiatives provide guidelines and expectations for increasing student reading proficiencies in five areas: phonemic awareness, phonics, vocabulary, fluency, and comprehension. Addressing mathematics is more complicated because there has not been an extensive, coordinated research effort in this content area. Rather, the research has been isolated for certain skills. The good news is that all states provide academic standards for development of math skills. According to the National Council of Teachers of Mathematics, which is often used as a resource for effective mathematics instruction, basic skills should be in conjunction with reasoning, problem solving, technology, and cross-disciplinary alignment. A valuable resource for examining essential mathematical skills is *Adding It Up: Helping Children Learn Mathematics,* which was published by the Mathematics Learning Study Committee of the National Research Council (Kilpatrick, Swafford, and Findell, 2001).

To ensure high-quality instruction, staff development should focus on specific skill strategies in the content areas as well as on the art of differentiating instruction. Teachers may need instruction, modeling, and feedback on how to increase academic instruction through flexible grouping, scheduling, and accommodation of different student learning styles. Since differentiated instruction strategies also rely on self-motivation, teacher training must include techniques for helping students develop intrinsic motivation.

The resources selected by the district's curriculum specialists should be included in the district framework to ensure consistency across campuses. Additional resources to build and support strong Tier 1 instructional practices include:

- *Guided Reading: Responsive Teaching Across the Grades* (Fountas and Pinnell, 2016)
- *40 Reading Intervention Strategies for K-6 Students* (McEwan-Adkins, 2010)
- *Visible Learning for Literacy: Implementing the Practices That Work Best to Accelerate Student Learning* (Fisher, Frey, and Hattie, 2016)
- *Implementing Guided Math: Tools for Educational Leaders* (Sammons, 2016)
- *Visible Learning for Mathematics: What Works Best to Optimize Student Learning* (Hattie, Fisher, and Frey, 2017)
- *Response to Intervention (RtI) and English Learners: Using the SIOP Model* (Echevarria, Richards-Tutor, and Vogt, 2015)

Universal Behavioral Interventions

Universal behavioral interventions are meant to be implemented school-wide. These interventions center on school-wide systems of supports that help students respond positively to their environment in the classroom. These supports include developing consistent classroom and school-wide rules and routines, teaching and modeling behavioral expectations, administering consequences fairly and consistently (both positive and negative), and ensuring that teachers are delivering effective and engaging instruction in their classrooms.

Positive behavioral supports are not a new concept. Many states require them as a part of the campus plan. Administrators and teachers must understand that

learning style The method of learning, individualized to a student, that allows the student to learn most easily and effectively.

intrinsic motivation Motivation that is governed by an individual's internal drives.

SIOP Model Sheltered Instruction Observation Protocol: An excellent resource for supporting the educational needs of culturally and linguistically diverse student populations.

positive behavioral supports are not a specific curriculum (although some excellent curricula support the system) and are not limited to a particular group of students. Effective behavioral supports in the school setting are foundational—they focus on the classroom and other specific settings (such as buildings, playgrounds, and buses) and on individual student needs. The campus administrator must analyze the universal screening data to ensure that the foundational pieces of behavioral supports are in place. If the data indicate gaps, they are then addressed through staff development.

prosocial behaviors Actions that are intended to benefit others in social situations.

> **Lessons Learned:** When a campus principal reviewed screening data at her elementary school, she found that four teachers generated 80 percent of the discipline referrals sent to her office. The principal and the RtI team conducted classroom observations and noted that classroom rules were not posted or reinforced, schedules and routines varied in the classrooms, positive incentives were not consistently given, negative consequences far outnumbered the positives, and students did not receive instructions or modeling of appropriate prosocial behaviors. The principal scheduled brief trainings on behavioral foundations for the teachers (three 45-minute trainings) led by the district's school psychologist. Training included developing classroom rules, using precision commands, and creating positive reinforcement systems in the classroom. Subsequent data collection showed a decrease in office referrals in all four classrooms.

Interventions that are proactive for behavior support include these:

Rules
- Predetermined, written, and posted
- Taught for at least the first 5 weeks of school
- Consistently monitored, with feedback for teachers
- Consistently enforced

Routines and daily schedules
- Posted
- Consistently followed
- Consistently taught

Consequences
- Predetermined
- Taught and arranged for more chances of receiving a positive support (Rule of thumb: Students should receive five positive consequences for

every negative consequence delivered.)
- Meaningful to the students (age appropriate)
- Given consistently and privately

Environment
- Organized
- Efficient
- Designed for maximum focus of attention
- Designed to increase student-teacher interactions

The most important aspect of universal behavioral interventions is related to teacher skills in the areas of designing organized classrooms (seating), setting schedules that are conducive to learning and behaviors (such as timing of instruction, seating, built-in breaks), managing the instruction by using groups and the environment, providing direct instructions regarding behavioral expectations that are tied to rules and social skills/character development, and implementing a good system of positive and negative consequences. A number of positive behavioral support systems offer direction for developing excellent school-wide structures, including, but not limited to, these two:

- CHAMPs (Sprick 1998)
- Project ACHIEVE

These additional resources related to universal behavioral supports are also recommended:

- National Association of School Psychologists (NASP) (www.nasponline. org)
- U.S. Department of Education Technical Assistance Center on Positive Behavioral Supports (www.pbis.org)
- Office of Special Education and Rehabilitative Services (OSERS) (www. ed.gov/about/offices/list/osers)
- Safe and Civil Schools (www.safeandcivilschools.com)

Tier 1 Integrity

One of the essential elements of a sustainable RtI process is the integrity of the Tier 1 instructional practices. The integrity of the system is often referred to in RtI literature as "fidelity." This simply means carrying out an instructional program in the manner in which it was designed. The RtI campus team will not be able to analyze data and provide supports if it cannot determine the appropriateness of the instruction within the classroom. Therefore it is crucial that the district provide staff development in the areas of assessment, instruction, and intervention to ensure fidelity.

Suggested practices to develop fidelity can be found at the National Research Center on Learning Disabilities website (www.nrcld.org). Basically, the district-level team must clearly outline the assessments to be used in the RtI process, devise a user-friendly format for presenting the data, articulate the interventions endorsed by the district, create a system for analyzing the data, and outline methods for accountability (particularly when intervention noncompliance occurs). According to the National Joint Committee on Learning Disabilities (2005), a three-dimensional model for fidelity of implementation includes providing a variety of tools for delivering information to staff, frequently checking to ensure fidelity, and using feedback and staff development to provide staff with the support they need to be successful.

The campus RtI team needs to use documentation to provide insight into the integrity of instruction in order to support the classroom teacher. This documentation must not be viewed as evaluative of the teacher; it is meant to provide data that are used to guide, coach, and support teachers with resources that help to maintain the integrity of the instructional process. Examples of documentation forms for Tier 1 analysis are located in Appendix B (Response to Intervention Team Documentation Forms).

To ensure monitoring effectiveness, it is very important for the campus RtI team to select a case facilitator/monitor to track consistency of implementation and staff behaviors as they relate to the design of the intervention and data collection. Generally speaking, when choosing the monitoring person, the team needs to evaluate who is trained in the specific area of instruction (reading, math, behavior), the instructional strategy used, or the intervention that is being observed. To ensure the validity of the observational data, the team must select a person who has been trained in structured observation techniques. The monitor must also possess effective consultation skills for providing positive corrective feedback to staff. And finally, the monitor must be someone the staff views with mutual respect.

It is crucial that staff be aware that this type of monitoring will occur as part of the RtI process and that it will be consistently implemented across all grades and teachers. When discussing the issue of monitoring for fidelity, the campus administrator needs to reassure the staff that this technique is part of designing high-quality supports and services and is not a punitive process. The staff need to be assured that the feedback is always given to the teacher in a collaborative manner after an observation and that it will be shared with the RtI team during its next regularly scheduled meeting.

structured observation technique A formal method of observing students within the school environment.

Chapter 4

Tier 2

*Matching Student Needs with Effective
Intervention Strategies*

In Tier 1 of RtI, instruction is based on aligning several data sources that naturally occur within the school district assessment calendar, classroom formative and summative data, and the universal screening information collected 3 times per year. Differentiated instruction is provided within the general education class. This level of instruction is applied to all students and is considered the least intensive for student support. Tier 1 focuses on having meaningful conversations that build strong evidence-based practices within the domains of instruction, curriculum, and environment, promoting grade-level success in the general education classroom.

Successful school districts monitor the learning rates of students with universal screening data, student products, and classroom observations. Students are identified as struggling learners based on these data and on documentation of the fidelity of research-based instruction, design, and strategies. The campus RtI team supports teacher efforts through feedback, training, and other resources.

After receiving Tier 1 instructional supports, some students may continue to struggle academically and/or behaviorally. Their learning rate falls below the preset cutoff score on universal benchmark data and data generated by the teacher (student products such as completed worksheets, homework, and projects; classroom observations; and teacher-made tests). For these students, the next step is to schedule a meeting, invite parents and appropriate staff, and consider the need for additional instruction within Tier 2.

In Tier 2 the added instruction layered on top of Tier 1 instructional supports (interventions) becomes student-centered and should be laser-focused on foundational skills necessary for success on the student's identified instructional level. This added layer of instruction is individually tailored to meet the struggling

campus RtI team A campus-level team of teachers, counselors, administrators, and support personnel who meet on a regular basis to discuss data-based instructional solutions for students who are demonstrating difficulty progressing on grade-level content within the general education setting.

foundational skills A set of skills students must master before they can become fluent in reading or math.

student's needs. The Tier 2 process relies on problem solving by the campus RtI team, which bases its decisions on assessments of student progress.

The Problem-Solving Process

The problem-solving process for intensifying student-based interventions begins at Tier 2. A good way to think of this phase is in terms of the student support teams of the past that addressed referrals for struggling learners. The main difference in the RtI process is that this stage is not considered a step toward special education eligibility. Instead, Tier 2 focuses on intervening early, before a problem becomes substantial.

It is important for parents and staff to understand that RtI is a general-education process and is not designed to categorize children into programs or to assign labels that define the problems or interventions. Rather, the Tier 2 process defines the problem objectively (as specific deficits in foundational skills in academics and/or behavior), uses the problem-solving method to create a plan of research-based interventions, collects data systematically, and evaluates the effectiveness of the plan.

Successful campus RtI teams must be actively involved in the problem-solving process as soon as it is determined that a student is in need of additional Tier 2 strategies, instruction, and intervention. Parents, staff, an administrator, or the campus RtI team may initiate a request for a meeting to discuss the data necessary to determine if a student is in need of this next stage of intervention. A meeting to discuss Tier 2 should be scheduled based on data collected and reviewed in Tier 1. These data should demonstrate that the student has already received an appropriate research-based curriculum and supports. If data are not brought to the meeting, then it is imperative that the meeting be rescheduled. Too many errors occur in the problem-solving process if inaccurate or incomplete data are used to make decisions and to plan focused student-based interventions.

focused student-based interventions Interventions designed for individual students that are focused on specific foundational skills necessary for student learning.

Lessons Learned: Current campus-based RtI teams continue to err and make decisions primarily based on emotions or feelings (teacher frustration, parent concerns, student struggles), particularly when teachers believe they have tried everything they know and nothing has worked. To determine whether a past decision was based on emotions or data, a team can look over the documentation to see whether it recorded opinions or facts. Solutions driven by emotions are detrimental because the supports chosen for a student often are misguided, causing correct and important interventions to be delayed.

Often the outcome of emotionally driven decisions is a premature referral for special education assessment, and the resulting tests indicate that the student does not meet eligibility standards for special education placement (often referred to as Did Not Qualify, or DNQ). It is important to note that this assessment can take many hours to complete, during which the student loses instructional time he/she cannot afford to lose. Not only does the assessment itself take time but the process is also lengthy, which may result in a loss of preventive interventions that could have been in place. Often when the special education assessment is initiated, the student does not continue to receive intensified differentiated instruction in Tier 1 and loses time in Tier 2 and 3 interventions. The unintended consequence of the premature referral (and of the teacher's mistaken assumption that the only appropriate intervention is special education) is that the integrity of the tiered process is compromised. This also can confuse the parents, because they were led to believe the correct intervention would be special education supports, only to be told that it was not a viable option because the student does not meet the criteria. When a campus RtI team uses data, this scenario can be avoided.

It is critical that decisions for moving students between Tier 1 and Tier 2 be consistently applied across all campuses in a school district. This is why a district-suggested framework is most important to sustain a strong RtI problem-solving process. It is easy to base decisions on emotions rather than data. Campus RtI teams work for the best interest of the child, and it is only human that emotions affect their decision making. Thus it is essential that the campus team be highly trained in the problem-solving process and adhere to the guidelines established by the district RtI team. (See Chapter 2 for details of establishing and training campus teams and developing guidelines for them.)

To improve student performance, problem solving needs to be comprehensive in evaluating the curriculum (what is being taught), the instruction (how it is being taught), the environment (the context in which learning is occurring), and the learner. An organizing framework for this analysis, referred to as RIOT/ICEL, is recommended by Hosp (2006). The data are organized within a table format (table 4.1) in which the top horizontal row includes the sources of data collection (RIOT: review, interview, observe, test). The left column includes the domains of learning to be reviewed (ICEL: instruction, curriculum, environment, learner). The data in these domains will help to explain the degree to which teacher-differentiated strategies and accommodations, curriculum demands/

Table 4.1. RIOT/ICEL data collection format

Domains of Learning	Sources of Data Collection			
	Review	Interview	Observe	Test
Instruction				
Curriculum				
Environment				
Learner				

resources, environmental influences, and learner-specific variables affect the student's ability to demonstrate growth. Using this as a guide, the team enters multiple data sources into the appropriate sections to aid in providing a comprehensive summary of the learner. (See the RIOT/ICEL matrix in Appendix E.)

Rule of thumb: Always let the data drive the decision-making process (figure 4.1). The steps in problem solving for struggling students are as follows:

1. Identify the problem by using available data to determine the skill deficit.
2. Interpret the assessment data to determine which specific areas need to be addressed, according to the student's learning and behavior rates.
3. Develop a plan that specifies interventions, outcome goals, fidelity checks, progress-monitoring methods, and the parties responsible for implementing the plan.
4. During implementation, evaluate the effectiveness of interventions by analyzing progress-monitoring data. If students have responded positively, continue the plan; if not, revise the plan and determine if added support is needed.

(Also see the RtI Implementation Guidelines for Problem Solving at the end of this chapter.)

Problem Solving versus Standard Protocol

standard protocol Interventions that match a set of research-based practices to students who show predictable patterns of performance.

In RtI, problem solving tailors interventions in order to change student outcomes (performance), while a standard protocol approach relies on interventions that are standardized. The standard protocol approach is more rigid, but it is not distinctly different from the problem-solving approach outlined above. The problem-solving method is more flexible in designing interventions to meet individual student needs, whereas the standard protocol model uses regimented interventions that are not flexible in how they are delivered to the student.

Strong sustainable systems successfully train their campus-based RtI teams to integrate both approaches in their framework. For example, research-based strategies for differentiated instruction and behavioral support tend to be more flexible when addressing Tier 1 concerns and strategies. On the other hand, the more rigorous additional instructional interventions of Tiers 2 and 3 may need to be highly structured, skill focused, and scripted to ensure integrity of the developed RtI plan designed for the student.

When the campus RtI team begins the shift to Tier 2, with added interventions and supports, the recommended focus is on standard protocol interventions. This focus not only will ensure fidelity of implementation but also will help with resource allocation. From the standpoint of financial and resource allocation, it can be very beneficial to the district to select three research-based interventions

**Step 1: Problem identification
(universal screening)**

Is there a problem?
What is the problem?
Why is it happening?

**Assessment:
universal
screening,
diagnostics, and
progress
monitoring**

**Step 4: Progress monitoring
(evaluate learning rate)**

Did the interventions work?
Are other interventions needed?

**Step 2: Determining
instructional level
(progress monitoring)**

Where in the curriculum is there a
match with student needs?

**Step 3: Intervention planning
and implementation**

What research-based
interventions match student
needs?
How can they be implemented?

Figure 4.1. The problem-solving
method of RtI. Note that each step
relies on data gathered through
several types of assessments.

for each of these areas: reading, math, writing, and behavior. The district can train interventionists on these specific programs and strategies and then use the trained personnel to deliver Tier 2 support or to coach/train teachers on appropriate use of the resources. This approach enables the campus administrator to track the fidelity and validity of the interventions more easily.

interventionists Persons trained in specific aspects of academic and behavioral interventions.

The Use of Multiple Data Sources to Monitor Academic Progress

The term "progress monitoring" is commonly misunderstood within the RtI process. There are essentially two types of progress monitoring. The Tier 1 type uses formative, summative, criterion referenced, norm referenced, and diagnostic data to drive conversations that focus on grade-level progress. The Tier 2 type is defined as frequent measurement of student progress in a brief, repeatable, reliable, and valid way. The difference between the two types is best explained in terms of the outcomes. Tier 1 monitors the progress on state standard outcomes expected of all students. Tier 2 focuses on determining whether a student is responding to an intervention. This distinction is important because the monitoring conducted in Tier 2 or 3 does not give teachers data that inform their classroom instruction; rather, it gives the team a compass to determine whether the chosen intervention is promoting student growth on specific foundational skills.

Data from Tier 2 progress monitoring enable the campus RtI team to evaluate student growth over time. This type of assessment detects even small advances

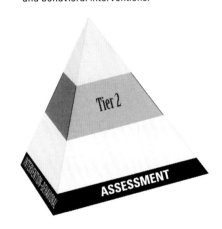

progress monitoring Frequent measurement of student progress in a brief, repeatable, reliable, and scientifically valid way; usually performed at predetermined intervals to allow for timely modification of instructional design to suit the student's needs.

**curriculum-based measurement
(CBM)** Any set of assessment
procedures that use direct observation and recording of a student's
performance in a local curriculum
to gather information for making
instructional decisions.

skill deficit A deficiency in a skill
that is necessary for learning to
occur or for achieving competence
in a given area.

probes In terms of progress
monitoring and curriculum-based
measurement, refers to brief
repeated assessments of an
academic skill.

instructional effectiveness A
measure of a teacher's delivery
of instruction, based on the
positive learning outcomes of
students.

delivery of instruction The methods for introducing information to
students.

retention rate A measure of a
student's ability to retain and
demonstrate a previously learned
skill.

in skill development and generally uses a measure of fluency (for instance, correct words per minute as a measure of reading fluency). The most typical kind
of progress monitoring is often referred to as curriculum-based measurement,
or CBM. This research-based assessment method is highly sensitive to the slightest skill development, can be administered quickly over short periods of time, is
performed frequently, and can report results in charts and graphs that are easy
for teachers, parents, and students to understand. It is important to emphasize
that when the RtI team meets to discuss student progress, monitoring data from
both tiers are necessary to determine student grade-level growth (Tier 1) and
instructional-level growth (Tier 2 outcome goal).

The purpose of Tier 2 assessment is to determine whether the chosen interventions succeed in advancing learning rates in the student's skill deficit areas.
This assessment will guide the team in problem solving for student progress. The
recommended schedule for administering CBM assessment in Tier 2 is twice
weekly, beginning at the onset of the intervention. The assessment results are
charted immediately after the administration, and then preset learning-rate rules
(discussed below) are used to determine whether the student is making progress.

CBM is essentially a set of various timed techniques (also referred to as probes)
that are elegant in the simplicity of their design, grounded in common sense (it
tests what is being taught), and heavily supported by research. CBM assessment
consists simply of repeated timed probes using readily available materials (it is cost-
efficient), employs standardized administration and scoring techniques (to ensure
technical adequacy—that is, consistent and reliable scoring), systematically monitors instructional effectiveness, and requires minimal training (it is easy to do).

The underlying philosophy driving CBM is to begin intervening at the point
where the student, especially the struggling learner, is in the curriculum—not
where the current curriculum is being taught. Instructional matching is the
key to identifying the starting point of the intervention. The campus RtI team
must know where to enter into the curriculum for delivery of the instructional
intervention and must use the appropriate pace of delivery of the instruction.
The assessment information allows the team to match the learner with tasks that
are appropriately challenging and that provide a realistic opportunity for success.

Many research studies over the past 30 years have documented the usefulness
of CBM. Stanley Deno (1987) defined CBM as any set of measurement procedures that use direct observation and recording of a student's performance in a
local curriculum as a basis for gathering information to make instructional decisions. CBM uses fluency measures to provide information for determining the
rate of skill acquisition, which is simply identifying the pace of teaching that is
best for the student. CBM also gives information regarding retention rate—that
is, the ability of the student to retain information that has been taught and to use
it in a meaningful way. Typically these rates are useful in identifying what types
of interventions may be needed for a student.

The most critical phase of implementing progress monitoring is the training of persons who will be administering, interpreting, and charting the data. Teachers follow a designated procedure and schedule for progress monitoring, administering measures at least twice a week. The assessments themselves are appropriate to the curriculum in which the intervention is occurring (including grade level). Teachers must know how to chart the resulting data. All staff involved must also be trained to analyze the data with regard to instructional effectiveness, so that they can use the information in their decision making. Parents will also need to be informed on how the assessment works. This can be accomplished by providing information through campus newsletters, meetings of the parent-teacher organization, and parent trainings.

CBM data link student performance directly to the curriculum and also enhance the academic success and continuous progress of students. The classroom teacher is led by the information to examine the curriculum and decide where entry levels begin for appropriate instruction and intervention. Then the teacher can match meaningful content to the student's instructional level and prior learning. These elements are critical to giving the student an appropriate margin of challenge that allows learning to occur.

An intervention plan based on CBM enables the student to use and build on prior knowledge. Working at an appropriate instructional level allows the student to feel comfortable and competent, which also increases motivation to learn. And the student can adjust the pace of learning to suit himself or herself, because the information provided is not too hard to process.

peer-assisted learning A specific research-based intervention that uses class-wide peer tutoring techniques developed by Doug and Lynn Fuchs.

Lessons Learned: Peer-assisted learning is a standard protocol procedure that can serve as an effective learning strategy for Tier 2 intervention. This technique allows peers to work with struggling learners in areas of needed support. Many districts that have strong sustainable Tier 2 interventions in place have designed and invested in peer tutoring as a Tier 2 instructional support. Students can be nominated by teachers and then trained to participate in the program. After being trained in research-based instructional strategies and CBM, the tutors are scheduled to work with identified students. They are also trained to document progress using CBM. This type of structured intervention program is very successful when implemented correctly and can be a valuable resource that is evidence-based and cost-effective.

Measurement tools used in CBM involve specific skills in the areas of reading, math, spelling, and writing. The oral reading probes are given individually to students in a quiet location. Reading probes generally allow 1 to 2 minutes for administration. The reading skill to be assessed is identified, and a probe for the skill is randomly chosen, such as phoneme segmentation. The student sits opposite the examiner, who has a numbered copy of the probe to score and follows a script to give directions. The student then begins to read aloud until the examiner says, "Stop." The examiner times the oral reading with a stopwatch. There are specific scoring criteria. A fluency rate (accuracy and speed) is determined from the score. The student is given three probes during the assessment. The examiner chooses the median (middle) score of the three probes and then asks the student to plot the score on a graph. By plotting the progress-monitoring chart, the student becomes part of the problem-solving process.

Many struggling learners do not have good learning habits or strategies, because they are overwhelmed with struggling in a curriculum that is not on their instructional level. When asked to plot the CBM scores within his or her instructional level, the student then can problem-solve aloud with the teacher about strategies that may be working or not working. This increases the student's motivation significantly.

positive reinforcement The process of associating a desired behavior with a desired consequence, which then increases the probability that the behavior will be repeated.

> **Lessons Learned:** Curriculum-based measurement can be a powerful motivator for those students who exhibit both reading difficulties and behavior problems (caused mostly by their attempts to avoid reading tasks). Students can provide their own positive reinforcement when they participate in graphing their own progress.

In math, students are asked to answer as many items as possible in 2 to 6 minutes on single-skill or multiple-skill computation probes that are designed to assess fluency of basic skills. On probes that measure concepts and applications of higher-order math skills, the time limits are 6 to 8 minutes. Math CBM probes can be given individually, to a small group of students, or to the whole class. The probes are scored immediately, and the student enters the score onto a graph. Fuchs and colleagues (2006) have identified expected learning-rate norms for mathematics.

In the area of written language, the student is given a lined composition sheet with a story starter sentence. The student is instructed to think for 1 minute about what he or she is going to write, and then is given 3 minutes to write the story. The story is scored for accuracy, grammar, sentence structure, and punctuation. The score is given to the student, who charts it on a graph.

Graphing of the data is done by plotting the number of correct words, letters, or problems on the vertical axis of the chart by the date of probe on the horizontal axis. The first CBM scores to be collected are called the baseline data

Table 4.2. The first- and second-grade oral reading fluency standard reported by Hasbrouck and Tindal (2017)

Grade	Percentile	Words Correct per Minute (WCPM)			Average Weekly Improvement (Learning Rate)
		Fall	Winter	Spring	
1	90	—	97	116	1.2
	75	—	59	91	2.0
	50	—	29	60	1.9
	25	—	16	34	1.1
	10	—	9	18	.56
2	90	111	131	148	1.2
	75	84	109	124	1.3
	50	50	84	100	1.6
	25	36	59	72	1.1
	10	23	35	43	.56

points. Baseline data points indicate where the student's instructional level is within the curriculum before the intervention begins. The baseline data points (3 probes) are plotted on the graph, and the median (middle) score is chosen as the beginning point of measurement for progress. This median point is then marked with an X and becomes the basis for all comparisons to determine whether the student is making progress from an intensified intervention.

Next, the team meets to decide on what the student's outcome goal (predicted skill level) will be, based on the intervention. Guidelines have been developed for expected learning rates (pace of skill acquisition). One such published set of reading norms for first through eighth grades can be found in research reported by Tindal, Hasbrouck, and Jones (2005). The norms include averages of expected words correct per minute (WCPM) at the start of the school year, as well as the expected average weekly gains when students are given instruction. This is important because decisions regarding intervention will be based not only on overall fluency scores but also on expected gains when instruction matches student needs. A norm table such as one from Hasbrouck and Tindal (2017) is used to predict learning goals (table 4.2).

The RtI team must determine the goal for the student's intervention by first selecting a target date to review the progress monitoring. Once that date is determined (typically 6 to 9 weeks within Tier 2), the team multiplies the number of weeks of intervention by the improvement rate selected from published norms for reading and writing. (Written language and spelling norms are not mandated, but they are sometimes needed.) That number is added to the baseline rate to obtain the outcome goal.

baseline data point An initial score that indicates a student's skill level before intervention; serves as the starting point in curriculum-based measurement of the student's response to the intervention.

outcome goal The targeted goal of an intervention plan.

Progress-Monitoring Graph for Reading

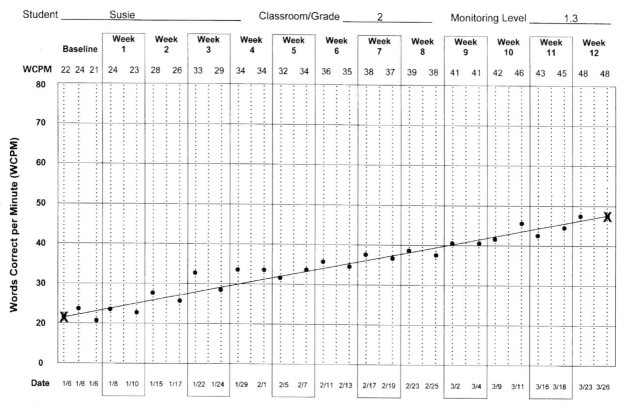

Figure 4.2. Example of a progress-monitoring graph. Solid circles indicate the student's median score of words correct per minute (WCPM) for each date of CBM administration. The X at the lower left marks the student's starting data point, and the X at the right marks the outcome goal on the last administration day. The straight line between the Xs is called the aimline. This student's data indicate that her progress is appropriate to the outcome goals defined in the aimline. The team's decision to continue the current intervention is appropriate. *Source:* Adapted from Intervention Central (www.interventioncentral.org).

Example: Emily is a fourth grader who read 84 words correctly per minute at baseline in a second-grade (Winter–January assessment) reading passage. A reasonable improvement rate for her would be a gain of 1.6 words per minute per week. The intervention team determined that the period of intervention was going to be 9 weeks.

9 weeks × 1.6 words gained per week = 14 words expected gain
84 words correct per minute (baseline) + 14 words correct per minute expected gain = 98 words correct (outcome goal)

The team next prepares to monitor progress by designing its own graph or by choosing a scoring graph from one of the resources mentioned above. To set up a progress-monitoring graph, label the horizontal axis with the dates of the CBM administration (typically by weeks of intervention) and the vertical axis with the CBM skill measure, such as words correct per minute in multiples of 5 or 10 (for a sample graph for a 12-week monitoring period, see figure 4.2).

The graph should be labeled with the student's name and the skill area to be measured. The first points to be recorded on the graph are the student's baseline data. Typically the student's three baseline data points are recorded, with the median score (middle) marked with an X to denote the starting data point. Next, place an X on the graph at the intersection of the final day of intervention on the horizontal axis and the outcome goal on the vertical axis. Then draw a line connecting the baseline data point to the outcome goal. This line represents the aimline for judging progress. The progress monitoring continues by plotting the median score for each administration on the graph.

The RtI team uses a set of decision rules for determining whether changes are needed in the student's intervention program. The research suggests using a data-point decision rule (Wright 2006). This rule should be applied after a minimum of six data points have been charted (not counting the baseline data points). The basic data-point decision rule is this: If three points are below the aimline, change the intervention. If three data points are above the aimline, adjust the aimline. And if the consecutive data points are falling within expected rates of growth, continue with the current program.

aimline A visual representation (line) on a progress monitoring graph that connects the baseline data point to the outcome goal.

data-point decision rule A means of interpreting curriculum-based measurement data (points on a graph) in order to make decisions about a student's intervention plan.

Lessons Learned: Samantha is a student who was referred for Tier 2 intervention. Her teacher reported she was reading within the beginning of the first-grade reading book (WCPM = 32). The team knew that in order for Samantha to be progressing, she needed to be improving her reading fluency to close the widening gap between her reading ability and that of her peers. The team determined that she should be reading 60 WCPM in the first-grade reader. The average expected learning rate increase for a first-grade reader is 2 WCPM, so the team decided that at the end of the 9-week intervention period Samantha would need to show a gain of 18 WCPM to demonstrate intervention success.

The team added the 18-word expected improvement to Samantha's baseline rate of 32 WCPM to arrive at an outcome goal of 50 WCPM by the end of week 9. If Samantha's progress-monitoring data demonstrate that rate at the end of the intervention period, the data will support the effectiveness of the intervention. Next the team determined the intervention that would be used to increase Samantha's reading fluency rate and developed the plan to clearly articulate the measurable outcome goals based on these data.

Finally, the team assigned the person responsible for implementing the intervention and documenting the progress monitoring. Each week, Samantha will be given the CBM measure for the correct instructional level (grade 1), and the score will be plotted on the graph. The data-point decision rule will be applied to the charted points to determine whether a change in the intervention is needed.

Districts may wish to use the wealth of information provided at Intervention Central (www.interventioncentral.org) for developing CBM in reading, writing, and math. Commercially developed CBM assessments that are available for districts to use include these:

- AIMSweb (www.aimsweb.com)
- Dynamic Indicators of Basic Early Literacy Skills (DIBELS) 6th Edition
- DIBELS Next
- IDEL (Spanish DIBELS)
- easyCBM
- Istation
- Measures of Academic Progress (MAP)
- STAR 360, Renaissance Reading and Math
- System to Enhance Educational Performance (STEEP)
- RAPS 360
- Texas Primary Reading Inventory (TPRI)

The National Research Center on Learning Disabilities has identified valuable resources for principals and teachers to support progress monitoring (Johnson et al. 2006). The center recommends the following resources for district personnel:

- Monitoring Basic Skills Progress (MBSP) (Fuchs; www.proedinc.com)
- Read Naturally (www.readnaturally.com)

Behavior Data Analysis

emotional disturbance eligibility Qualification of a student as eligible to receive special supports to counteract a chronic behavior or emotional condition that adversely affects his or her educational performance.

functional behavioral assessment A collection of information about events that predict and maintain a student's problem behavior; used to construct a behavior action plan.

Tier 2 analysis of social, emotional, and behavioral data focuses on systematic data collection and interpretation for use in designing strong social, emotional, and behavior supports. It is important to note that IDEA 2004 did not change the criteria for emotional disturbance eligibility. The data collected in Tier 2 are used to verify that a problem continues to exist by objectively defining the social, emotional, or other behavior of concern and to prioritize the concerns. Then realistic and achievable criteria for success can be specified.

The philosophy behind Tier 2 data collection and analysis is that such data allow the staff to understand the context in which a problem behavior is occurring. Objective behavioral data analysis moves staff away from a reactive, consequence-based approach toward the identification and teaching of appropriate alternate social, emotional, and positive behaviors. The purpose of this data collection is to identify important relationships among a set of targeted social skills or appropriate behaviors for a particular student. Social, emotional, and behavioral data can also identify multiple underlying causes that contribute to the expression of the problem behavior.

Conducting an analysis of social skills, attentional skills, and behavioral skills results in five primary outcomes:

1. Operational description of the identified social skill or behavioral needs
2. Identification of events, times, and situations that predict when a social skill or problem-solving behavior deficit occurs across a range of typical daily routines
3. Identification of the functions and consequences (positive or negative) of the presenting inappropriate social skill or behavior
4. Creation of a hypothesis statement of what is happening to contribute to the problem
5. Design of interventions using specific research-based training in social and behavior skills

Behavioral progress monitoring is also used to determine effectiveness of the interventions. Data sources for Tier 2 behavioral data analysis include a review of student records:

- Discipline referrals
- Behavior incidents
- Classroom and school-wide observations
- Teacher interviews
- Student self-assessments
- Attendance records
- Parent interview

Additional data are collected to help the RtI team objectively define the problem behavior in the context of the settings in which it occurs, including the intensity, frequency, and duration of the behavior. The teams should focus on building empathy and social skills and should use the universal screening data from the behavioral screener to target skills to address. The data should document all Tier 1 Positive Behavioral Interventions and Supports (PBIS) interventions, any previous individual interventions attempted and their outcomes, as well as the impact the negative behavior or social skills deficit has on student learning and classroom disruptions. The assessment should not focus only on negative behaviors, however. It should also identify the student's academic and behavioral strengths.

The first step of the behavioral analysis is to define the behavior of concern or

problem behavior Behavior that has been identified as impeding the learning of the student or of others in the student's environment.

consequence What happens immediately after a behavior occurs.

operational definition A description of behaviors that are observable and measurable.

the social skills deficit in operational and measurable terms. This means that the behavior or social skill should be described in such a way that anyone who reads the description clearly understands what the behavior or social skill looks like. For instance, "off task" is not an operational definition. However, "stares down at feet," "taps pencil on desk," and "touches peers' papers" are good examples of operational definitions of behavior.

Step two is to collect data specific to the identified deficit in social skill or problem behavior. The data should be collected across settings and people. It should also identify instruction, curriculum, and environmental factors associated with the problem behavior. Another helpful piece of data is called a setting event—an event that is removed in time from the occurrence of the problem behavior but is related to it. Setting events may include medications, sleep cycles, eating routines and diet, daily schedules, staffing patterns and interactions, academic tasks, and social demands.

setting event An event that is removed in time from the occurrence of a problem behavior but is related to it.

Next, the reason for or function of the behavior is identified. Most often the function is to get something or to avoid something. Research indicates, however, that functions of behavior will vary if the student has underlying problems with emotional regulation, increasing the likelihood that the function is more than just to escape or obtain something. Areas to consider when a student is suspected of having underlying emotional conditions may include emotional reactivity due to depression, anger, or anxiety; distorted thought patterns; reinforcement due to environmental triggers; modeling of inappropriate behaviors; family issues; developmental disabilities; functional communication needs; and the educational setting (environmental factors).

environmental triggers Events or situations in the student's environment that bring about a behavioral response.

It is not possible for the RtI team to analyze the behavioral data without understanding the context in which the problem behavior occurs. The data provided by Tier 1 documentation are very helpful at this stage. Also, the problem behavior may have more than one function or social skill deficit attached to it.

functional communication The use of language in a meaningful and understandable way.

Once the RtI team identifies the behavior's function or social skill deficit, the next step is to generate a hypothesis statement. This statement is related to the defined function of the problem behavior or the absence of a social skill and includes the behavior and the conditions under which it occurs.

hypothesis statement In the functional behavioral assessment, the statement that identifies the function that maintains a student's problem behavior (what the student gets out of the behavior).

Lessons Learned: The RtI team met to discuss George's problem behavior as documented by his teacher. The team reviewed all data and generated the following hypothesis statement:

When George has spent the weekend at his noncustodial parent's house and he is presented an independent task without visual cues or prompts on the Monday morning after the visit, he demonstrates passive noncompliance by placing his head down on his desk to avoid completing the task.

The team's hypothesis statement can be broken into the following elements:
Setting event: George spends the weekend at his noncustodial parent's house
Antecedent event (trigger): He is presented with an independent task without visual cues or prompts on the Monday morning after the visit

Behavior: He demonstrates passive noncompliance (head down on desk)
Function: To avoid completing the task

passive noncompliance The failure of a student to perform a teacher's request, often by acting as if he or she did not hear it.

antecedent event An event that triggers a problem behavior.

The fifth step in functional behavioral assessment begins with designing the intervention. The RtI team generates a list of possible alternate behaviors. In order for the intervention to be effective, the alternate behaviors must achieve the same function that the problem behavior does. For example, if the problem behavior's function is to avoid a task, then the alternate behavior must also provide the opportunity to avoid the task.

Lessons Learned: Susan was a third-grade student who consistently threw her math worksheets (double-digit subtraction with regrouping) on the floor when her teacher gave her the task. Assessment information indicated that Susan was working on her instructional level; however, she needed more time than most students to complete tasks. Susan's worksheets were modified by giving her 5 problems to complete at a time instead of 20 problems per worksheet. She was placed on a positive behavior support system that required her to complete the 5 problems without throwing the paper on the floor. She would then earn the opportunity to place an X over one problem on the next worksheet (effectively allowing her to earn the right to avoid one problem). This system worked very well for Susan, and within 3 weeks she was no longer demonstrating the avoidant behavior of throwing her worksheets on the floor.

positive behavior support system A systematic approach that clearly establishes behavioral expectations and uses reinforcement when the student demonstrates appropriate behaviors.

When designing interventions to recommend based on the functional behavioral assessment data, the RtI team should focus on three areas:

Instruction: Identify current instructional levels, and match academic interventions to instructional needs.
Behavior: Identify positive behavior support plans and strategies to train and shape appropriate behaviors.

Environment: Modify the environment to increase the likelihood of positive learning and behavior outcomes.

The following questions may help focus the recommendations on these three areas:

What are the curriculum demands and the student's current skill level?

What types of specific interventions would lead to an increase in the alternate behaviors?

What type of environment would lead to a decrease in the inappropriate behavior?

Finally, the RtI team needs to decide on appropriate data collection techniques for progress monitoring of social, emotional, and behavioral interventions. The most common type of direct assessment of behavior involves systematic observations. For assessment of social skills acquisition, the most common type of data collection is observation during role-play situations first and then observation of generalization of skills in the classroom.

A skilled and trained observer must observe the behavior in natural settings, classify the behavior objectively as it occurs, ensure the reliability of the observation, and convert the information to quantify occurrences of the behavior. According to Jerome M. Sattler (2002), skilled observers are trained to distinguish behaviors in operationally defined terms. They sustain attention during the observation and focus on details in the environment. Skilled observers are able to document behaviors efficiently and are able to summarize data in succinct terms. (See the RtI Classroom Observations Form in Appendix B.)

direct observations Systematic, structured observations that use well-designed observation record forms.

The primary objective of using direct observations is to keep the data collection simple. RtI team members need to be trained on how to select times for conducting observations—such as choosing an activity that is compatible with the occurrence of the target problem behavior, selecting a variety of times and settings for observation, and choosing times when the student is likely to demonstrate a variety of behaviors. Training includes helping observers focus on specific details when special circumstances occur during the observation such as a fire drill, a substitute teacher, or peer misbehavior.

The following are examples of questions that can be asked during a direct observation in the classroom:

Does the student engage in the target problem behavior with one teacher but not another?

Does the target behavior occur at school but not at home?

Does the target behavior occur in the morning but not in the afternoon?

There are several methods that can be used to record direct observations:

Anecdotal recording: Maintaining a simple running record and account of what is happening in the environment. This account can be handwritten, keyed in on a computer, audiotaped, or videotaped.

Interval recording: Dividing observations into brief segments (15–30 minutes). The observer tallies the presence or absence of the defined target problem behavior during the discrete time period.

Event recording: Recording each instance of the target problem behavior as it occurs throughout an observation period.

ABC: Documenting <u>a</u>ntecedent event (what happens before), <u>b</u>ehavior (occurrence of the target problem behavior), and <u>c</u>onsequence (what happens immediately after the behavior).

In addition to collecting data through direct observation, the RtI team needs to review records to identify any factors that may contribute to the occurrence of the problem behavior, such as issues at home, in the community, or at school, as well as disabilities. Poverty and language barriers may be contributing factors. Interactions between parent and child and other social interactions may also affect behavior progress.

Measurement should focus on the reduction of the targeted problem behavior as well as the occurrence of the taught alternate behavior. Fidelity of implementation of the positive behavior support system is essential for behavior change. Campus staff must also understand that behavior change takes time, and they should not rush to judgment within a brief period of time (i.e., less than 6 weeks).

Strategic Interventions: Academic

Strategic interventions at Tier 2 provide additional focus on foundational skills for the student (instructional level, not grade level). This intensified level of intervention is designed for students who have not made progress within the curriculum and instructional strategies provided in Tier 1. When data analysis of multiple sources identifies students who need Tier 2 interventions, those students also continue to receive Tier 1 supports and curriculum. The Tier 2 interventions are delivered in small groups of no more than 5 students. The RtI team designs the intervention to occur a set amount of time per week, depending on the resource used for the intervention, typically an additional 60 to 90 minutes of instruction per week. The interventions are implemented by the classroom teacher or any other trained staff. Typical duration of interventions at this stage is 6 to 9 weeks (repeated as needed, but not to exceed 18 weeks).

Tier 2 interventions are designed with individualized goals for each identified struggling learner. The interventions are research-based, and progress monitoring occurs weekly during the intervention phase.

The most important aspect of selecting interventions at Tier 2 is that they be aligned with the data collected in Tier 1. The RtI team should analyze the student's data to determine whether a deficit is skill-based or performance-based. The intervention plan must determine and chart the outcome goals that have been defined specific to the student's academic skill deficit, and it should include who will intervene, when the intervention will occur, and what resources are needed for success.

Interventions must also meet research-based standards as defined in ESSA and IDEA 2004 (refer to the discussion of these standards in Chapter 3, "Universal Academic Interventions"). Some helpful websites review intervention resources:

- Best Evidence Encyclopedia (www.bestevidence.org)
- Florida Center for Reading Research (www.fcrr.org)
- National Research Center on Learning Disabilities (www.nrcld.org)
- Reading Rockets (www.readingrockets.org)
- What Works Clearinghouse (ies.ed.gov/ncee/wwc/)

Additional research-based Tier 2 interventions include, but are not limited to, the following:

Reading

- Fast ForWord (Tallal; www.scilearn.com)
- Fountas and Pinnell Leveled Literacy Intervention (LLI) (fountasandpinnell.com/lli)
- Istation (istation.com)
- Mindplay Virtual Reading Coach (mindplay.com/student-programs/virtual-reading-coach/)
- Open Court (SRA/McGraw-Hill; www.mheducation.com)
- Peer-Assisted Learning Strategies (PALS) (Vanderbilt Kennedy Center for Research on Human Development; vkc.mc.vanderbilt.edu/pals)
- Plato Learning (www.plato.com)
- Read 180 (Scholastic; teacher.scholastic.com/products/read180/)
- Rigby Literacy (rigby.harcourtachieve.com)
- Stepping Stones to Literacy (Sopris West; www.voyagersopris.com)

Writing

- Write Well (Sopris West; www.voyagersopris.com)

Mathematics—elementary

- Everyday Mathematics (SRA/McGraw-Hill; www.wrightgroup.com)

Mathematics—middle school

- Connected Mathematics (Pearson Prentice Hall; connectedmath.msu.edu)
- I CAN Learn Pre-Algebra and Algebra (JRL Enterprises; www.icanlearn.com)

skill deficit A deficiency in a skill that is necessary for learning to occur or for achieving competence in a given area.

performance deficit An inability to demonstrate a skill that has been learned.

- Mathletics (us.mathletics.com)
- Neufeld math curriculum (www.neufeldlearning.com)
- Saxon Middle Grades Math (Saxon; saxonpublishers.hmhco.com/classroom

It is important to note that Tier 2 interventions are not necessarily computer-assisted programs or additional curriculum resources. An intervention may be focused skill instruction such as *Cover-Copy-Compare Worksheets for Students.* When first introducing Cover-Copy-Compare worksheets to the student, the teacher gives the student an index card. The student is directed to look at each correct item on the left side of the page; for example, a correctly spelled word or a computation problem with the solution:

Vocabulary: The student is instructed to cover the correct model on the left side of the page with an index card and to write both the word and its definition in the space on the right side of the sheet. The student then uncovers the correct model on the left to check his or her work.

Math: The student is instructed to cover the correct model on the left side of the page with an index card and to copy the problem and compute the correct answer in the space on the right side of the sheet. The student then uncovers the correct answer on the left and checks his or her own work.

Another example of focused skill instruction is referred to as "incremental rehearsal of sight words." A student is presented with flashcards containing unknown items added to a group of known items. Presenting known information along with unknown allows for high rates of success and can increase retention of the newly learned items, behavioral momentum, and resulting time on task. Research shows that this technique can be used with sight/vocabulary words, simple math facts, letter names, and survival words/signs. In addition, this technique could be used for other facts, such as state capitals or the meanings of prefixes or suffixes.

Strategic Interventions: Behavioral

Even when solid positive behavior support systems are in place on a school-wide basis, some students (5 to 10 percent) will need additional strategic interventions that are individualized to their needs. Tier 2 social, emotional, and behavioral interventions are intentionally designed and are best developed for small groups (no more than 5 students). Such interventions are frequently monitored. (See the RtI Social, Emotional Behavior Action Plan form at the end of this chapter.) Although individual students will need strategic interventions for social skill

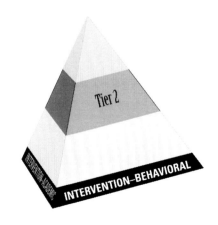

acquisition and decrease of problem behaviors, it is important to note that positive behavior support interventions are not a specific curriculum nor are they limited to a certain group of students.

Each of the strategic behavioral interventions at Tier 2 has the following characteristics:

- The intervention is readily available.
- It is implemented by the appropriately identified support staff (most often the general education counselor within a small group social skills situation).
- It is consistent with the school-wide positive support plan.
- It is driven by the behavior analysis data reviewed by the RtI team.

Tier 2 strategic interventions should also improve the structure of the student's environment by tailoring it to the student's individual needs, and they should provide for frequent feedback and increased opportunities for success. Interventions should be designed to be implemented across all settings (they should be easy to do in classes and common areas such as the cafeteria, halls, and playground), to link the behavior supports to academic supports, to include opportunities for positive reinforcement, and to teach self-management skills.

A wide variety of interventions can be incorporated in a strategic behavior action plan at Tier 2. Education (training and instruction), skill building, self-monitoring, and reinforcement can be combined to devise effective interventions, such as the following, to address particular problems.

Stress inoculation: Teachers train students to use coping skills when they are frustrated with social or learning situations. The students are taught to focus on needed skills, rehearsing them and then applying them in the school or home setting.

Proactive intervention and insight training: Students learn to recognize behaviors that cause distress in their environment, and then they problem-solve ways to modify or change the behavior. This type of training is very helpful for students who experience behavioral issues related to depression and anxiety.

Anger management training: Students learn strategies to help themselves reduce emotional and physical responses to stressful triggers of anger. Anger management training also teaches students to use thinking rehearsal strategies to promote problem solving for dealing with frustration and stressful events.

Parent training: Parents are given helpful tips for managing their children's behavior at home. This strategy is proactive, focusing on suggestions to help prevent the problem behavior in the first place.

Behavior contracting: A contract is developed with the student that relates to work completion or designates appropriate behaviors within the classroom.

Social skills training: Training focuses on the skills needed for successful social interactions, such as entering into a conversation or asking for help.

Precision command requests: Requests are delivered by using a series of non-emotional commands in a consistent manner that allows the adult to maintain control of the situation. This technique is very helpful with students who demonstrate high levels of noncompliance.

Behavioral momentum: The student is asked to do two or three things he or she is likely to do (preferred activities), in order to create a positive behavior flow before a request is made for a behavior that the student is less likely to do.

Behavior rehearsal: The student is taught the desired behavior and then is given opportunities to rehearse it in the natural classroom setting.

Peer-initiated modeling: The student's peers are taught how to demonstrate specific behaviors that are required to complete a desired task. The peers then serve as role models for the student. While they all are completing the desired activity, the teacher gives the student corrective feedback paired with positive reinforcement to promote behavioral and academic skill acquisition.

Group contingency system: In this reinforcement strategy, the whole group (the class) must meet a desired outcome or standard before a positive reinforcement is given.

Reinforcement token economy system: This positive behavior support strategy is proactive by encouraging good behaviors with incentives. When students demonstrate a desired behavior, they earn a token, which can be saved and redeemed later for a reinforcer (such as extra time on the computer, a homework pass, or lunch with a favored teacher).

Excellent resources for developing social, emotional, and behavioral intervention strategies are available, including the following:

- Intervention Central (www.interventioncentral.org)
- Positive Behavioral Interventions and Supports (PBIS; www.pbis.org)
- Project ACHIEVE (www.projectachieve.info)
- Ripple Effects (rippleeffects.com)
- Safe and Civil Schools (www.safeandcivilschools.com)

To summarize, these are the keys to developing a good behavior action plan:

1. Modify events before the problem behavior occurs (setting events, antecedent events).
2. Teach the student the new alternate behavior that is expected to replace the problem behavior.

3. Increase and improve the positive consequences the student receives for demonstrating the positive alternate behavior.

4. Strengthen the consequences for demonstrating the problem behavior.

5. Continuously evaluate the plan using identified behavior recording techniques.

Lessons Learned: The most common problems arising from the implementation of Tier 2 academic and behavioral strategic interventions have involved districts and campuses that did not define cutoff scores or establish data-point decision rules to monitor student progress. In addition, when interventions were not clearly defined or implemented with fidelity at Tier 2, campuses experienced difficulties related to the problem-solving process because the campus RtI teams were reluctant to conduct fidelity checks. Some of the most critical problems occurred when RtI teams did not effectively document their intervention plans or progress monitoring.

To avoid these problems, follow the procedural guidelines in this book for setting up the RtI process, and then evaluate the consistency with which documentation, fidelity checks, and corrective feedback are used by the campus RtI team. When there is consistency in delivering the Tier 2 process, extraordinary progress can be made with even the simplest academic and behavioral interventions.

RtI Implementation Guidelines for Problem Solving

1. **Gather information.**
   a. Appointed RtI team member meets with teacher and explains process.
   b. Teacher provides referral information supporting indicators (emotional and behavioral) of struggling learners, as well as academic data (benchmarks, student progress, Tier 1 interventions in place, and outcomes).

2. **Identify the problem.**
   a. Appointed team member establishes baseline data using CBM.
   b. Appropriate staff member (e.g., school psychologist, counselor, social worker) consults regarding emotional or behavioral issues.
   c. Focus on the problem, not the solution—describe problem(s) in objective, measurable terms.
   d. Rank-order concerns, and set measurable goals based on learning-rate norms.

3. **Brainstorm solutions.**
   a. Discuss district resources aligned with specific research-based strategies that could be used with identified problem(s).
   b. Encourage input from all team members, including parents.
   c. Generate as many solutions as possible.

4. **Evaluate interventions.**
   a. Identify strategies to be used (modify or combine brainstormed solutions).
   b. Check for referring teacher's agreement.
   c. Use collaborative feedback and shared decision-making.

5. **Choose intervention strategies.**
   a. Align strategies with appropriate tier (Tier 2 or 3).
   b. Review criteria for determining acceptable progress.

6. **Develop action plan.**
   a. Designate who is responsible of implementing and monitoring each strategy.
   b. Establish timelines, and set follow-up meeting time.
   c. Monitor intervention effectiveness using data from continuous progress monitoring (CBM and behavioral measures).
   d. Continue, modify, or add interventions based on student progress data.

RtI Social, Emotional Behavior Action Plan

Name: _____ Grade: _____ School: _____ Date: _____

Goal (based on target behaviors and replacement behaviors identified in Functional Behavioral Assessment)

_____

This intervention plan will address the following:

_____ Antecedents   _____ Behavioral Skill Deficits   _____ Academic Skill Deficits   _____ Positive Reinforcement   _____ Consequences

_____ Crisis Intervention   _____ Environmental Changes   _____ Other

The following research-based interventions and strategies will address this function: _____

Specific Interventions and Strategies	Person(s) Responsible	Revisions (Include date)

Identify dates for evaluation of student's progress toward goal:

Behavior to be measured	Baseline Data (Quantitative)	Goal	Review Date & Behavioral Data	Review Date & Behavioral Data	Review Date & Behavioral Data	Review Date & Behavioral Data	Review Date & Behavioral Data

Tier 3 and Beyond

Intensifying Interventions When Learning Rates Do Not Improve

Tier 3 in the RtI process is designed for students who have significant difficulties making progress, despite receiving Tier 1 and Tier 2 interventions. Tier 3 provides the most intensive and individualized interventions to the student. The main difference between Tier 3 and Tier 2 is that Tier 3 interventions are more frequent and of longer duration, and either the group size is reduced or the student receives the intervention individually.

As the RtI team collaborates with teachers and parents to provide strategic interventions for students within Tier 2, progress monitoring drives their decision making. The campus RtI team monitors the student progress data for the amount of time the district guidelines recommend, usually 6 to 9 weeks. At the designated time—9 weeks, for example—the RtI team meets, reviews progress, and then uses the district's framework for decision rules to decide whether (a) to continue with Tier 2 interventions for another 9 weeks because the student is demonstrating progress, (b) to return the student to Tier 1 because he or she has made significant gains, or (c) to increase the intensity of intervention to Tier 3. Typically, approximately 5 percent of the students on a campus will need intensified Tier 3 interventions (not including already identified special education students).

It is important to note that shifting into Tier 3 does not automatically generate a referral for Section 504 committee support or for special education eligibility. Rather, Tier 3 signals intensifying the interventions while monitoring the student's progress to determine whether resources need to be adjusted. If a student's learning rates have not accelerated after the predetermined amount of time (4 to 6 weeks), then the RtI team considers whether the student needs additional services, such as special education.

Section 504 committee A school-based team that meets to discuss the needs of a student with a disability condition and how the condition affects learning. (Section 504 is a federal law that prohibits discrimination against individuals with disabilities.)

More Monitoring of Academic and Behavioral Progress

Assessments of learning and behavior at Tier 3 continue as designed in Tier 2, using CBM and behavior charting to monitor progress. However, the RtI team may increase the progress monitoring to twice a week.

Behavioral assessment may include updating the data on the acquisition of social or behavioral skills that occurred within Tier 2. After analyzing the student's social skills or behavior charts, the RtI team may decide that the social skill group focus or the individual behavior action plan needs to be modified or that additional supports are needed for the development of social, emotional, or behavioral skills.

More Intensive and Individualized Interventions

The interventions at Tier 3 may be the same programs that were used in Tier 2 (individualized instruction to build skills or the standard protocol). The difference is in the intensity of the interventions. For instance, if the student was receiving additional reading instructional interventions 3 times a week for 30 minutes each in a small group of 4 or 5 students, in Tier 3 the student would receive the intervention 5 times a week for 30 to 45 minutes per session, individually or with no more than 3 other students.

Also important to note is that the student in Tier 3 continues with Tier 1 interventions. This means that the student remains in the general education classroom for initial instruction with a differentiated approach (Tier 1), and the student receives the Tier 3 interventions at a designated time during the day.

The most important administrative support needed at this level is the flexible scheduling of general education and intervention support staff, in order to accommodate the intensive interventions of Tier 3. Remember that only about 5 percent of the student population on the campus will fall within Tier 3. Therefore the number of students needing this level of intervention will not overwhelm the RtI team and campus staff.

The district RtI team may want to add another intervention at Tier 3, in addition to using intensified Tier 2 interventions. To do this, it is recommended that the district team develop a standard protocol of interventions from which the campus teams can choose (for details, see "Problem Solving versus Standard Protocol" in Chapter 4). Like all RtI interventions, those in the protocols are identified according to research-based standards. Having a protocol helps streamline training and resource allocation, and it aids in the fidelity of implementation. For these reasons, using a standard protocol approach for selecting targeted interventions at Tier 3 makes sense.

Lessons Learned: One school district developed a standard protocol that specified that Tier 2 students may receive one of the following intervention resources for reading: Istation individualized lessons, Fountas and Pinnell LLI (Leveled Literacy Intervention), or Reading A-Z (Spanish). The district also identified one Tier 3 reading intervention, Mindplay Virtual Reading Coach. The district then trained interventionists and select staff on each campus on how to implement these interventions. The data revealed that a total of 175 children received the Tier 2 reading interventions and 69 children additionally received the Tier 3 intervention. Of the 69 children who received the Tier 3 intervention, 26 did not demonstrate sufficient progress and were referred for special education assessment.

Three Tiers or Four Tiers?

There has sometimes been confusion regarding how special education and Section 504 services fit into the RtI model. Think of these services as being on the continuum of service delivery. If a student continues to show a significant lack of progress in learning rate despite all of the Tier 2 and 3 interventions—and the fidelity of the intervention plan has been documented—then that evidence would indicate that referral for additional services needs to be considered.

There has also been much confusion as to where special services are located on the RtI continuum of service delivery. Remember that moving a student into Tier 3 does not automatically generate a referral for a multidisciplinary assessment. To avoid any confusion, some districts follow a four-tier RtI model in which Tier 4 is identified as special education.

RtI and Special Education Identification

Response to Intervention is not designed to be a pre-referral process. It is not a model in which students must "fail" before interventions begin. Instead, it is a proactive, positive approach for supporting all learners, particularly those who are struggling. RtI meets the students where they are within the curriculum and positively affects their learning rates. To accomplish this, RtI uses research-based interventions that have known positive effects on struggling students. Research has shown that when students are engaged in the curriculum on their instructional level, many of them will respond positively without the need for Tier 3 interventions.

Although the RtI process may take longer to refer students for special education assessment than the traditional pre-referral approach does, the students are already receiving intensive individualized instruction and interventions begin-

individualized education plan (IEP) Either the educational program to be provided to a child with a disability or the written document that describes that program. Public schools are required by IDEA to develop an IEP for every student with a disability who meets the federal and state requirements for special education.

learning disability As defined by IDEA, "a disorder in one or more of the basic psychological processes involved in understanding or in using language, spoken or written, that may manifest itself in an imperfect ability to listen, think, speak, read, write, spell, or do mathematical calculations, including conditions such as perceptual disabilities, brain injury, minimal brain dysfunction, dyslexia, and developmental aphasia." Learning disabilities do not include "learning problems that are primarily the result of visual, hearing, or motor disabilities, of mental retardation, of emotional disturbance, or of environmental, cultural, or economic disadvantage" (34 CFR 300.8).

educational diagnostician A professional with an ability to assess and diagnose the learning problems of students.

ning at Tier 2. Think in terms of the struggling learner at Tier 3. If this student is referred for special education and qualifies for it, naturally the goals and objectives of the individualized education plan (IEP) will closely match what is already occurring on the RtI team's intervention plan (although the intensity and allocation of services will change). Additionally, students who receive special education as their Tier 3 intervention must also continue receiving Tier 1 supports. Therefore these students remain in the general education class for differentiated instruction in their skill deficit areas and then receive their Tier 3 special education support at another time. It is important for parents and educators to understand that even if a student is identified as eligible for special education because of a learning disability or a behavior problem, the general education classroom teacher remains the teacher of record, and the special education staff (using Tier 3 interventions outlined on the IEP) support the general education staff in achieving positive outcomes for the student.

The movement toward an RtI process for identification of learning disabilities occurred because research showed that many children were incorrectly identified as having a learning disability when in fact they had not received strong instruction. The idea behind the RtI process is simple: if the students are given access to the research-based instructional practices that are proven to be effective for struggling learners, then the learning rates for the students will show positive outcomes without the need of specially designed instruction.

If a district is going to develop a solid RtI process intended to aid in the identification of learning disabilities, the staff will need training in areas such as these:

- Interpretation of universal screening
- Collection and interpretation of progress-monitoring data (CBM)
- Quality assurance regarding the fidelity of research-based instruction, strategies, and interventions
- The use of standard protocol interventions selected at Tiers 2 and 3

When a district is preparing to implement RtI as part of its process to identify learning disabilities, the campus staff must clearly understand whose responsibility it is to collect and document assessment at each tier. Tier 1 assessment using universal screening is the responsibility of the general education classroom teacher for all students. However, it is also the responsibility of special education staff, educational diagnosticians, and school psychologists to consult with the general education staff on reviewing and interpreting the universal screening data.

The quality of the general education instruction and strategies is verified and documented by classroom teachers, support personnel, and the RtI team. The campus administrator is responsible for overseeing issues relating to fidelity and for providing support and resources as needed.

Progress—both academic and behavioral—is monitored by teachers, trained personnel, and members of the RtI team. The resulting data are interpreted by special educators, educational diagnosticians, and school psychologists.

The RtI team is responsible for problem solving to select Tier 2 and 3 interventions that are based on research and outlined in the district's guidelines for RtI and identification of learning disabilities. The team is also responsible for documenting interventions and the fidelity of their delivery.

The assessment for special education is completed by trained and certified staff, such as educational diagnosticians, speech and language pathologists, and school psychologists. Because the RtI process continuously assesses student progress and needs, it contributes the data necessary for the special education eligibility assessment.

All districts are required to conform with state and federal regulations regarding eligibility determination under the IDEA 2004 mandate. According to federal standards, eligibility criteria should include information that identifies effective interventions. The data must be generated from multiple sources, and a variety of assessment methods must be used. Assessment must also take into consideration cultural, socioeconomic, racial, family history, language, and educational variables.

Eligibility for special education continues to be decided by a team of professionals and parents (the IEP team). Team members include a representative of the local education agency (generally the school district), parents, the general education teacher, a special education teacher, assessment personnel who can interpret the instructional implications of the assessment results, and others who have appropriate knowledge regarding the student and/or the disability condition. The data for the team's decision making include information that was collected during the RtI process, as well as the results of the special education full and individual evaluation.

IEP team The group of people responsible for developing, reviewing, and revising an individualized education plan.

Within the federal requirements for special education eligibility, as specified by IDEA, are factors that are considered "exclusionary" to eligibility. A student will not be judged eligible for special education if one of these factors is identified as the primary reason for lack of progress:

- Lack of appropriate instruction in reading or math
- Limited English proficiency
- Cultural or economic disadvantage

full and individual evaluation A comprehensive set of data gathered from multiple sources for each student being considered for special education and related services.

In order for a student to be eligible for special education, the data collected must establish both the presence of a disability and the need for special education support or related services.

Educational progress is the focus of RtI, and progress data that are objective and linked to the intervention are essential. Progress-monitoring data that are important to establishing eligibility include baseline data collected before the intervention; measurable goals derived from the baseline data; the learning rate, as documented on the intervention plan developed by the RtI team; and evaluation of the progress-monitoring data. The progress-monitoring data should include a comparison of the expected performance (outcome goal) and the measured performance (learning rate plotted on a CBM chart) during the intervention period. (For details, see "The Use of Multiple Data Sources to Monitor Academic Progress" in Chapter 4.)

learning difference A difference between the student's performance and that of typical peers or expected standards.

The next question to ask is whether there is a difference between the student's performance and that of typical peers or expected standards (learning-rate difference). This issue is very complex and is defined according to state standards. IDEA 2004 allows states to *prohibit* the traditional approach of using a severe discrepancy between intelligence and achievement scores as the sole criterion for identifying a learning disability. The regulation also specifies that states cannot require the use of intelligence and achievement score discrepancy for determining learning disabilities. Also according to IDEA 2004, states are *required to permit* the use of a process (RtI) to determine whether a student responds to research-based intervention.

According to the National Association of State Directors of Special Education (NASDSE 2005), eligibility for special education is determined by integrating data collected from multiple sources that document the level of difference between the student's performance and that of peers. These sources include benchmark data (universal screening), learning-rate differences based on improvements (progress-monitoring data, as charted against an aimline), documentation of a need for special education (how the student's learning is negatively affected by the skill deficit), and ruling out the exclusionary factors listed above.

All students are afforded protections under the IDEA 2004 requirements for assessment, procedural safeguards, and due process. Parents have the right to be informed, and their permission for assessing a student's special education eligibility must be obtained. Two aspects of this process should be addressed in relation to RtI: requests from parents to have their children assessed for special education eligibility, and independent evaluations of student eligibility for special education.

Parental Request for Evaluation

Parents have the right to request that their child be tested for a suspected disability under Section 504 (the most common disability is dyslexia) or for special education eligibility. This request may present a problem if prior documentation is not available regarding the student's exposure to research-based instruction, interventions used, and progress charting to identify whether a learning-rate difference exists. It is suggested that when a parent makes a request, the RtI team should review the request and the student's records. The team then examines the student's current instructional levels and assessment data (from universal screening, benchmarks, and classroom products). If it determines that the student has an educational need, the team may elect to start Tier 2 interventions and progress monitoring, or it may determine the need for Tier 3 interventions and assessment. If the progress-monitoring data are not available when the parent makes the request, the data must be collected. Communication between the RtI team and the parents is essential. If the parents believe that the only way their child can be successful is by categorizing or labeling the child, then the team has not done its job in explaining the RtI process. Parents need to be assured that the label does not drive the intervention and that their child will receive the necessary supports, regardless of a classification. It is vital that both staff and parents understand that identification of a learning disability needs to include progress-monitoring data that have been collected and reviewed.

Keep in mind that when a parent requests an evaluation of the child's eligibility for special education, the school district must either conduct the evaluation or give the parent written notice of its refusal to do so. A parent may request an evaluation prematurely, when Tier 1 and/or Tier 2 interventions have not yet been tried. In such a case, written notice of refusal may be appropriate, but it must be done properly, in compliance with the law and regulations.

Independent Educational Evaluations

A parent has the right to request an independent educational evaluation (IEE) if the parent disagrees with the evaluation conducted by the school. The IEE process begins when a parent requests, in writing, an assessment that is conducted by an independent agent. A difficulty arises if the independent agent does not consider or have access to the RtI data: universal screening, interventions, and progress monitoring. It is essential that the district provide this information to the independent agent for consideration. The district should have a process in place that makes the data available to the independent agent. It is the responsibility of the independent agent to use and interpret the data appropriately in the context of the evaluation, and this may be problematic if the agent is not familiar with how to analyze the data in a meaningful way. The IEP team must consider the extent to which the independent agent used and interpreted the data to generate his or her conclusions and recommendations.

independent educational evaluation (IEE) As defined by IDEA, "an evaluation conducted by a qualified examiner who is not employed by the public agency responsible for the education of the child in question" (34 CFR 300.502).

Lessons Learned: One campus conducted the RtI process along with the special education assessment process and determined that a particular student was not eligible for special education, based on two factors: the learning-rate difference was not significant when the student's progress-monitoring graph was analyzed (that is, the student demonstrated progress with intervention); and multiple measures used in the standardized assessment yielded consistent average or low average scores, which did not indicate that the student was demonstrating a learning disability. Additionally, campus personnel had documented excessive absences and tardies for the student. Campus staff were concerned that the student had not been afforded access to instruction, because of absences and the excessive tardies. An intervention plan was recommended to increase the student's attendance and access to the reading instruction, with extra tutorials and interventions. Progress-monitoring data revealed that when the student was present in class, his learning rates increased. Based on the data, the IEP team decided that Tier 2 interventions were appropriate and that special education eligibility had not been established.

The parent disagreed with the team's decisions and requested an independent educational evaluation. The team gave the independent psychologist all relevant data pertaining to the student, and the psychologist's assessment results were consistent with those from the district's assessments. However, the psychologist did not use the progress-monitoring data or the school records of tardies as part of her evaluation, and she concluded that the student was indeed eligible for special education services because he was not passing his classes.

The campus IEP team invited the psychologist to the IEP meeting to go over the evaluation results. After much discussion, the psychologist admitted that the current intervention plan proposed by the team was appropriate and the eligibility criteria for special education had not been established. The psychologist also commented that she needed to "take some classes" to help her understand the RtI process and not immediately shift to a "categorizing mentality" when evaluating the needs of struggling students.

Reevaluation

Many questions have been asked about how reevaluations are conducted for students already identified as having a learning disability. Progress monitoring during Tiers 2 and 3 should continue and should be documented on the IEPs. The objective and goals of the IEPs should flow from the interventions and assessments that are part of the RtI process. Therefore reevaluation data can be derived from the progress monitoring and the documentation of learning rates. If a student who is receiving special education demonstrates progress on learning rates, the IEP team determines whether the student is ready to exit special education and move into less intensive support or should remain in special education with updated goals and objectives. The critical determination is to establish whether the student continues to demonstrate a need for special education services.

Epilogue

The past 11 years of consulting and training on RtI has resulted in many successful outcomes for school systems, students, parents, and individual teachers across the United States. Many school systems that were struggling to achieve acceptable growth for all students have successfully revisited philosophies, readjusted staff and schedules, and streamlined resources with positive results as measured by their data. Student growth continues to climb dramatically in the overhauled systems, parents feel more welcome as partners in the process, and thousands of teachers have reported personal growth in their teaching methodologies.

Focusing on a process that aligns data, excellent teaching methodologies, and parent and staff involvement clearly shows results in the form of extraordinary prospects for student growth. When you encounter bumps and challenges along the way—and you certainly will—remember that readjusting and realigning your current practices will take time. Go slow, be patient, and above all continue with a razor-sharp focus on the individual student, and you will never be disappointed.

Appendix A

Frequently Asked Questions

Some common questions often come up when I consult on the Response to Intervention process. Here are the ones that seem to be foremost on the minds of most educators.

What is Response to Intervention?

Response to Intervention is practicing high-quality instruction and interventions that are matched to student needs. Ongoing assessment is used to monitor student progress on a frequent basis and to make important educational decisions.

Is this just another referral process defined by special education law?

No. Actually RtI was born out of the No Child Left Behind Act of 2001, which moved to improve accountability within the schools in order to promote adequate yearly progress for all children. The IDEA 2004 provisions of new guidelines for identification of learning disabilities aligned federal special education expectations to the No Child Left Behind Act, specifically with regard to the importance of a Response to Intervention model as part of the eligibility decision making.

What is the multi-tier model?

The multi-tier model is represented by a three- or four-tier paradigm. Tier 1 represents approximately 80 percent of all students, with all curriculum, instruction, and supports provided within the general education setting. In Tier 1 the most common assessments are universal screening and curriculum-based assessments. For those students (approximately 20 percent) who do not respond to Tier 1 curriculum, instruction, and supports, a team will provide Tier 2 interventions. In Tier 2, students receive individualized, intensive, research-based interventions in addition to Tier 1 supports and are assessed frequently using curriculum-based measurements. The students are monitored for a predetermined amount of time (typically 6 to 9 weeks, but no more than 18 weeks). Approximately 5 to 8 percent of students will show continued difficulty and a lack of progress, even with Tier 2 interventions. These students will then be provided Tier 3 interventions along with Tier 1 interventions. Tier 3 is simply an increase in the intensity of intervention (possibly with additional interventions) and the frequency of curriculum-based measurements.

If a student moves to Tier 3, does that trigger an automatic referral for special education services?

No. In fact, entry into Tier 3 is a continuation of data collection to determine if the increased intervention may jump-start learning. Data collection continues but intensifies, and the time for intervention is reduced to 4 weeks before the decision is made to continue intervention or to refer the student for special education assessment. Data collected during the first 4 weeks of Tier 3 can help the RtI team determine whether the student demonstrates progress or whether the student may need a comprehensive assessment to determine special education eligibility. It is important to note that a student may be referred for assessment *at any time* during the RtI process if the data indicate the need for individualized instruction or if the parent requests the assessment.

Who is responsible for deciding how RtI will work in my district?

Ideally I suggest that the district-level administrators (such as superintendent, curriculum coordinators, and special education administrators) work together to develop district guidelines. Once the guidelines are established, RtI then becomes a campus-based responsibility, with the campus administrator as the leader. The campus RtI team will be responsible for the RtI assessment, instruction, and intervention process.

What would be a good cutoff score for universal screening?

Ultimately the best way to determine a meaningful cutoff score is to develop local norms derived from curriculum-based assessments, but that takes time. A good guideline is to identify struggling learners as those students who fall below the 25th percentile on the instrument chosen for universal screening. One thing to consider is that the district may need to adjust the cutoff score after the first year's universal screening data have been gathered.

You have mentioned the importance of progress monitoring in this process. I understand the concept, but I want to know who will be responsible for administering the assessment.

The campus RtI team will determine the appropriate person(s) to carry out the progress monitoring. In Tier 1 all assessment is considered the responsibility of the general education teacher. In Tier 2, also, it typically is the classroom teacher who includes the additional progress monitoring assessments in the weekly data collection. Tier 3 assessments may be completed by a standing member of the team, the person responsible for the interventions, or a designated staff member trained in administering, scoring, and documenting the assessment.

My principal asked me to be on the team, but I am hesitant because I fear this is just one more thing for me to do. Will this be too much for me to handle with all my other extra responsibilities?

Team membership should be considered carefully by the teacher, while understanding that being asked to serve in such an important role is a positive reflection on the teacher. Team members should be respected for the amount of responsibility it takes to participate in and be an active member of the team. If you ever feel that this is an added burden, then your campus team should adjust its practices. It is recommended that the campus principal recognize the additional time and effort needed to be a team member, and honor that commitment by shifting the team member's current responsibilities to other staff.

What happens when a parent requests testing or when we get a prescription form requesting a test by a doctor?

All requests must be reviewed by the team immediately. The team has a responsibility to review all data and use the data in a consistent manner to make decisions. If there are data indicating that the child is struggling, the team needs to decide the level of intervention, develop specific interventions, and determine appropriate assessments. Remember that a parent request for an evaluation triggers a legal responsibility. The district must either conduct the evaluation or give a proper written notice of its refusal to do so.

Do you have a list of research-based interventions we should use?

Although there is not an exhaustive list, there are interventions that have met the standard. Interventions regarding delivery of instruction range from cooperative grouping and accommodation of learning styles to peer-assisted tutoring and differentiated instruction techniques. (See Appendix C, Online Resources.) There are also other interventions listed in this book that may aid you in the search. I recommend that the district first inventory all interventions already in place and review the literature to determine if those interventions meet research-based standards.

Appendix B

Response to Intervention Team Documentation Forms

RtI Team Documentation Checklist

Campus:_____Case Facilitator:_____

Student:_____Grade:_____Teacher(s):_____

Tier 1 Documentation (ongoing and completed every 6 weeks)

_____Review of universal screening trends - Dates:_____, _____, _____

_____Review of lesson plans in area of concern

_____Review of student work samples

_____Review of case facilitator consultation documentation

_____Review of classroom observations focusing on curriculum, instruction, environment, and learner

_____Review of fidelity checks

_____Review of 4 sources of assessment (screening, diagnostics, progress monitoring, outcomes)

Note: All sources of documentation are attached to the team meeting form used by the district.

Tier 2 Documentation (weekly progress monitoring and completed every 6 weeks)

_____Review of intervention design

_____Review of intervention alignment with diagnostic and progress-monitoring data

_____Review of student growth (Tier 1 grade level; include all formative assessments and student work samples)

_____Review of student growth (Tier 2 instructional level, measured by diagnostics and progress monitoring)

_____Fidelity checks on Tier 2 intervention

_____Team decisions regarding analysis of multiple sources of data, intervention status, and student support (change in tiers, etc.).

Note: These data are collected with the ongoing Tier 1 data collection.

Tier 3 Documentation (intensified weekly progress monitoring and completed in 4–6 weeks)

_____Review of intervention design

_____Review of intervention alignment with diagnostic and progress-monitoring data

_____Review of student growth (Tier 1 grade level); include all formative assessments and student work samples)

_____Review of student growth (Tier 3 instructional level measured by diagnostics and progress monitoring)

_____Fidelity checks on Tier 3 intervention

_____Team decisions regarding analysis of multiple sources of data, intervention status, and student support (change in tiers, etc.).

Note: These data are collected with the ongoing Tier 1 data collection.

Referral for Section 504 or Special Education Evaluation

_____Completion of district forms (include all RtI problem-solving information) - Date:_____

Essential Case Facilitator Responsibilities
for Consultation in Tier 1

1. **After universal screening has been administered,** the campus RtI team (of which the case facilitator is a member) completes the following tasks:
   a. Reviews the universal screening data on all students and analyzes trends.
   b. Makes team-member assignments for each of the students to be supported.
      i. Assigns the staff member (an administrator) who will be responsible for checking fidelity.
      ii. Assigns the staff member (other than the case facilitator) who will be responsible for student observation.
   c. Schedules and documents a teacher consultation to discuss the following (this consultation occurs no later than 1 week after the initial team meeting):
      i. Concerns about the student
      ii. Tier 1 strategies to address these concerns
      iii. How to accomplish the reading, math, or behavior documentation
      iv. Program-monitoring technique to be used

2. **Within a week after the teacher consultation,** the case facilitator meets with the student's teacher (or teachers) to do the following:
   a. Determine whether the teacher has begun implementing a Tier 1 strategy. If not, the case facilitator and the teacher problem-solve together to find out why not and what support the teacher needs (e.g., the facilitator assists the teacher with finding proper resources and/or informs the RtI team of the teacher's need for support).
   b. Determine whether the teacher has any questions regarding the strategies
   c. Determine whether the teacher needs any additional resources to implement the strategies
   d. Determine whether the teacher is still satisfied with the strategies designed. If not, the case facilitator and the teacher problem-solve together to minimally modify strategy and/or the case facilitator informs the RtI team.
   e. Update documentation to include additional information collected since the previous consultation.

3. The case facilitator checks with the student's teacher (or teachers) approximately **every 2 weeks for the duration of the intervention** and performs the following tasks:
   a. Determines whether the strategy and the program monitoring are being implemented as designed.
   b. Determines whether the teacher is maintaining the appropriate documentation
   c. Documents the conversations and any additional information provided by teacher
   d. Reports back to the RtI team regarding student progress.

RtI Team Documentation: Tier 1 Instructional Strategies for Increasing Academic Engagement Time

Teacher/Content Area: _____ Student: _____ Date: _____

Key Points	Salient Features	Consistency of Implementation	Fidelity Check
High-quality, research-based activities	Yes No Are aligned with state curriculum standards/content objectives. Yes No Are rigorous and relevant to content designed for high student interest and multisensory involvement. Yes No Provide students with choice of activity. Yes No Assess student age, interests, needs, learning styles, and developmental level when designing activity. Yes No Use a variety of activities in order to avoid practice effects and saturation, which can inhibit on-task engagement.	Attendance Work Samples Classroom Observations Notes:	Fidelity Check Classroom Observations Lesson Plan Review Notes:
Positive outcomes for students	Yes No Students take ownership in their learning. Yes No Student engagement increases when students are presented with activities based on their interest and ability level. Yes No Allowing for choice of product increases student motivation. Yes No Ability to build foundational skills increases when activity is individualized for students.	Attendance Work Samples Classroom Observations Notes:	Fidelity Check Classroom Observations Lesson Plan Review Notes:
Teacher planning	Yes No Review curriculum strands based on state expectations. Yes No Determine which materials and resources are necessary. Yes No Align activity with direct instruction embedded in lesson plans. Yes No Determine product assessment tool (e.g., rubrics) and evaluation methods. Yes No Plan for sharing with grade/content teachers.	Attendance Work Samples Classroom Observations Notes:	Fidelity Check Classroom Observations Lesson Plan Review Notes:

We assure that the above-noted intervention(s) were conducted as disclosed.

_____ _____ _____
Principal/ RtI Team Chair   Classroom Teacher/Service Provider   Case Facilitator

RtI Classroom Observations

Student:_____ Grade:_____ Date of Observation:_____

Teacher:_____ Campus:_____

Observer: _____ Time of Day: From_____ to _____

Teacher-Student Ratio:_____ Instructional Level of Lesson:_____

Time on Task: *(Circle* **on task [+]** *or* **off task [−]** *at 10-second intervals.)*

+ −	+ −	+ −	+ −	+ −	+ −	+ −	+ −	+ −	+ −	+ −	+ −	+ −	+ −	+ −

Class/Subject Observed: *(Observation should be in the area of suspected disability.)*

○ English/LA	○ Reading	○ History/Social Studies	○ Science
○ Math	○ Specials	○ Other:	○ Other:

Student-Teacher Ratio during Observation Period:

Students:	○ Fewer than 10	○ 10–15	○ 16–20	○ More than 20

Classroom Arrangement:

○ Rows of desks	○ Grouped desks	○ Tables	○ Centers	○ Other:

Classroom Interaction with Teacher:	Yes	No	Not Observed	Comments:
Demanded teacher attention	○	○	○	
Was attentive to instruction/instructor	○	○	○	
Had excessive concern with achievement	○	○	○	
Participated in class discussion	○	○	○	
Responded appropriately to: Praise	○	○	○	
Correction	○	○	○	
Required firm discipline	○	○	○	
Was out of seat without permission	○	○	○	

Work Behavior:				
Began tasks promptly	○	○	○	
Had short attention span	○	○	○	
Was easily distracted	○	○	○	
Appeared prepared and organized for activity	○	○	○	
Follows oral instruction	○	○	○	
Follows written instruction	○	○	○	
Works effectively in: Small group	○	○	○	
Large group	○	○	○	
Alone	○	○	○	
Appears to work to limit of ability	○	○	○	

Classroom Interaction with Peers:				
Interacts with peers appropriately	○	○	○	
Disturbed others: Frequently	○	○	○	
Occasionally	○	○	○	
Not at any time	○	○	○	

Comments:_____

_____

_____

Signature of Observer_____Position_____

RtI Documentation of Tier 1 Instructional Interventions: Basic Reading

Student: _____ Teacher(s): _____

Student Date of Birth: _____ Grade: _____ Date of Review: _____ Case Facilitator: _____

Targeted Area of Instruction	Instruction and Curriculum			Tier 1 Core Instruction Supports	
	Description of Participation in Core Curriculum (amount of time, mode of instruction, lesson plan objectives)	Has Student Been Provided Appropriate Core Curriculum?	Strategies (interventions)	Consistency of Implementation	Fidelity Check
Phonemic awareness		Yes No		Attendance Work samples Formative assessment	Fidelity check Classroom observations Lesson plan review
Phonics		Yes No		Attendance Work samples Formative assessment	Fidelity check Classroom observations Lesson plan review
Fluency		Yes No		Attendance Work samples Formative assessment	Fidelity check Classroom observations Lesson plan review
Vocabulary		Yes No		Attendance Work samples Formative assessment	Fidelity check Classroom observations Lesson plan review
Comprehension		Yes No		Attendance Work samples Formative assessment	Fidelity check Classroom observations Lesson plan review

We assure that the above-noted intervention or interventions were conducted as disclosed.

_____ _____ _____
Principal/RtI Team Chair Classroom Teacher/Service Provider Case Facilitator

RtI Documentation of Tier 1 Instructional Interventions: Reading Literacy

Student: _____   Teacher(s): _____

Student Date of Birth: _____   Grade: _____   Date of Review: _____   Case Facilitator: _____

	Instruction and Curriculum			Tier 1 Core Instruction Supports	
Targeted Area of Instruction	**Description of Participation in Core Curriculum (amount of time, mode of instruction, lesson plan objectives)**	**Has Student Been Provided Appropriate Core Curriculum?**	**Strategies (interventions)**	**Consistency of Implementation**	**Fidelity Check**
Fluency of text reading		Yes No		Attendance Work samples Formative assessment	Fidelity check Classroom observations Lesson plan review
Vocabulary (as defined as the breadth and depth of knowledge about the meaning of words)		Yes No		Attendance Work samples Formative assessment	Fidelity check Classroom observations Lesson plan review
Comprehension		Yes No		Attendance Work samples Formative assessment	Fidelity check Classroom observations Lesson plan review
Background knowledge related to content of text		Yes No		Attendance Work samples Formative assessment	Fidelity check Classroom observations Lesson plan review
Higher-level reasoning skills		Yes No		Attendance Work samples Formative assessment	Fidelity check Classroom observations Lesson plan review
Motivation and engagement for understanding and learning from text		Yes No		Attendance Work samples Formative assessment	Fidelity check Classroom observations Lesson plan review

We assure that the above-noted intervention or interventions were conducted as disclosed.

_____   _____   _____
Principal/RtI Team Chair   Classroom Teacher/Service Provider   Case Facilitator

RtI Documentation of Tier 1 Instructional Interventions: Written Language

Student: _____

Student Date of Birth: _____ Grade: _____ Date of Review: _____ Case Facilitator: _____

Instruction and Curriculum			Tier 1 Core Instruction Supports	
Targeted Area of Instruction	**Description of Participation in Core Curriculum** (amount of time, mode of instruction, lesson plan objectives)	**Has Student Been Provided Appropriate Core Curriculum?**	**Strategies (interventions)**	**Consistency of Implementation**	**Fidelity Check**
Writing content		Yes No		Attendance Work samples Formative assessment	Fidelity check Classroom observations Lesson plan review
Mechanics of writing		Yes No		Attendance Work samples Formative assessment	Fidelity check Classroom observations Lesson plan review

We assure that the above-noted intervention or interventions were conducted as disclosed.

_____   _____   _____
Principal/RtI Team Chair   Classroom Teacher/Service Provider   Case Facilitator

RtI Documentation of Tier 1 Instructional Interventions: Math

Student: _____ Teacher(s): _____

Student Date of Birth: _____ Grade: _____ Date of Review: _____ Case Facilitator: _____

Targeted Area of Instruction	Tier 1 Core Instruction Supports			
	Instructional Strategies (interventions)		Consistency of Implementation	Fidelity Check
Math concepts and problem solving	Explicit instruction	Y N		
	Multiple examples	Y N		
	Think-aloud approach	Y N	Attendance	Fidelity check
	Visual representations to problem-solve	Y N	Work samples	Classroom observations
	Use of multiple heuristic strategies	Y N	Formative assessment	Lesson plan review
	Peer-assisted instruction	Y N		
Mechanics of computation	Explicit instruction	Y N		
	Multiple examples	Y N		
	Think-aloud approach	Y N	Attendance	Fidelity check
	Visual representations to problem-solve	Y N	Work samples	Classroom observations
	Use of multiple heuristic strategies	Y N	Formative assessment	Lesson plan review
	Peer-assisted instruction	Y N		

We assure that the above-noted intervention or interventions were conducted as disclosed.

_____ _____
Principal/RtI Team Chair Classroom Teacher/Service Provider

_____
Case Facilitator

RtI Documentation: Tier 2/Tier 3 Intervention and Assessment

Interventionist: _____ Student: _____ Grade: _____ Tier: _____

Instructional Skill(s)/Level	Date	Day of Week	No. of Minutes	Progress-Monitoring Data
		M T W Th F		CBM probe level_____ WCPM _____ DCPM _____ BCPM _____
		M T W Th F		CBM probe level_____ WCPM _____ DCPM _____ BCPM _____
		M T W Th F		CBM probe level_____ WCPM _____ DCPM _____ BCPM _____
		M T W Th F		CBM probe level_____ WCPM _____ DCPM _____ BCPM _____
		M T W Th F		CBM probe level_____ WCPM _____ DCPM _____ BCPM _____
		M T W Th F		CBM probe level_____ WCPM _____ DCPM _____ BCPM _____
		M T W Th F		CBM probe level_____ WCPM _____ DCPM _____ BCPM _____
		M T W Th F		CBM probe level_____ WCPM _____ DCPM _____ BCPM _____
		M T W Th F		CBM probe level_____ WCPM _____ DCPM _____ BCPM _____
		M T W Th F		CBM probe level_____ WCPM _____ DCPM _____ BCPM _____
		M T W Th F		CBM probe level_____ WCPM _____ DCPM _____ BCPM _____
		M T W Th F		CBM probe level_____ WCPM _____ DCPM _____ BCPM _____
		M T W Th F		CBM probe level_____ WCPM _____ DCPM _____ BCPM _____

Abbreviations: WCPM, words correct per minute; DCPM, digits correct per minute; BCPM, behaviors correct per minute.

Appendix C

Online Resources

This is a list of online resources I have found most helpful when consulting with school district staff about Response to Intervention. Although this list is by no means exhaustive, it includes the resources necessary for developing and implementing a Response to Intervention model.

Leadership Characteristics for Administrators Who Are Facilitating Change
Center for Educational Networking: www.cenmi.org
Southwest Educational Development Laboratory (SEDL): www.sedl.org/
change/leadership/intro.html

Assessment
AIMSweb: www.aimsweb.com
Dynamic Indicators of Basic Early Literacy Skills (DIBELS): dibels.uoregon.
edu
easyCBM: easycbm.org
Intervention Central (CBM Warehouse): www.interventioncentral.org
Istation: Istation.com
Measures of Academic Progress (MAP): NWEA.org
RAPS360: Mindplay.com
Screening to Enhance Educational Performance (STEEP): www.isteep.com
STAR: Renaissance.com
Texas Primary Reading Inventory: www.tpri.org

Academic Interventions and Instructional Strategies
Access Center: Improving Outcomes for All Students K–8: www.
k8accesscenter.org
Florida Center for Reading Research: www.fcrr.org
Intervention Central: www.interventioncentral.org
Learning Styles: www.learningstyles.net
Peer-Assisted Learning Strategies (PALS): kc.vanderbilt.edu/pals/
Sheltered Instruction Observation Protocol (SIOP): cal.org/siop/
Strategies for Differentiating Instruction: members.shaw.ca/priscillatheroux/
differentiatingstrategies.html

Tips of Implementing Guided Reading Lessons: scholastic.com/teachersblog-posts/sharon-taylor/tips-implementing-guided-reading-lessons/

Vaughn Gross Center for Reading and Language Arts: www.texasreading.org/utcrla/

Visible Learning: visible-learning.org

What Works Clearinghouse: www.whatworks.ed.gov

Behavior Strategies and Interventions

BASC-2 Behavior and Emotional Screening System (BASC-2 BESS): personclinical.com

CBM Warehouse: www.interventioncentral.org

Character Counts!: www.charactercounts.org

National Association of School Psychologists: www.nasponline.org

Positive Behavioral Interventions and Supports: www.pbis.org

Project Achieve: www.projectachieve.info

Project Resilience: www.projectresilience.com

Social, Academic, and Emotional Behavior Risk Screener (SAEBRS): ebi.missouri.edu

Student Risk Screening Scale (SRSS): mibl.si.org/evaluation/student-assessment-risk-screening-scale

RtI Process

National Association of State Directors of Special Education: www.nasdse.org

National Research Center on Learning Disabilities: www.nrcld.org

Office of Special Education and Rehabilitative Services: www.osepideasthatwork/toolkit/ta_responsiveness_intervention.asp

Parents

LD Online: www.ldonline.org

Response to Intervention (RTI): A Primer for Parents: www.ldonline.org/article/15857 or nasponline.org/resources/handouts/rtiprimer.pdf

Appendix D

Multiple Sources of Data

Connecting Multiple Sources of Data

Is there evidence of access to instruction?
Universal Screening, Unit Assessment, District Benchmarks (Trends)
Student Product, Classroom Observations

YES **NO**

Instructional Level Differentiated Strategies

Comparison to Peers Focused skill gap instruction

Does the student meet the educational standards that apply to all students?
Description of instruction provided
Description of learning environment
District/classroom expectations and criteria for measuring progress/success
Individual achievement data
Student work samples/portfolios
Formative Assessment Data (checklists, observations, quiz scores, teacher notes)
Data about behavior, attendance, other factors
Background information, historical data
Comparative data of peer performance

YES **NO**

Continue instruction Multiple tiers of support for
focused skill remediation (Tiers 2-3)

Did the student respond to intervention?

YES **NO**

Continue Instruction Professional judgment: Design FIE

Converge Data
1. Did the student fail to respond to instruction/intervention?
Universal Screening (below 25th percentile)
Progress monitoring (ROI), student products
2. Rule out exclusionary factors
3. Are there domain-specific patterns of strengths and weaknesses?
RIOT data (RtI)
Diagnostic FIE Assessment

Is there a pattern of severe delay in classroom achievement in one or more areas that has existed over time?

Severe delay in classroom achievement means the student cannot do the same academic work as other students in the classroom even with reasonable general education instructional strategies (Tier 1) and supplemental interventions (Tiers 2 & 3).

Using Multiple Sources of Data

Strong problem solving involves the use of multiple layers of data to aid in instructional decision making. In addition to providing the information necessary to arrive at instructional decision making with regard to individual students, data serve to pinpoint specific student needs. The RtI team and classroom teachers should use assessment information to design instructional and behavioral intervention strategies that are likely to improve student learning.

Selecting Data to Analyze

In addition to the technical concerns, including test bias, select data tools that provide useful data. Effective data tools should possess the following characteristics:

- ✓ Are efficient, requiring minimal time to administer, and specific, pinpointing the specific problem under review.
- ✓ Are sensitive, revealing meaningful successive approximation and progress toward goals.
- ✓ Are easily interpreted, yielding accurate information about a student's performance that can be clearly communicated to others.
- ✓ Provide documentation, resulting in a succinct record of the data.
- ✓ Provide data that have instructional utility, which can be readily translated into specific goals, short-term objectives, and intervention plans.

Data Sources

The foundation of the team interpretation skills lies in the three basic abilities: analytic looking, listening, and asking (Hargrove & Poteet, 1984). Even the best assessment tool cannot accomplish the goals of sound evaluation unless the assessors themselves possess the following characteristics:

- ✓ Knowledge of district and state curriculum standards and performance benchmarks
- ✓ Knowledge and skill in a wide variety of ways to collect information in a classroom setting, including structured observation
- ✓ An understanding of valid indicators of effective classroom environments
- ✓ Working knowledge of effective instructional strategies
- ✓ Awareness of the need to match important learning skills and outcomes with assessment strategies used to measure them
- ✓ Ability to select assessment instruments and strategies that will provide valid and reliable data
- ✓ Understanding of test administration procedures and adherence to them during testing
- ✓ Skill in interpreting assessment data in meaningful and practical terms
- ✓ Capability of clearly communicating data results in language understandable to teachers and parents during meetings

Source: Adapted from training materials designed by Gail Cheramie and Andrea Ogonosky, for professional guidance and use, 2016.

Useful data from multiple sources can be summarized as:

Beneficial (good evidence)	Less clear (weak evidence)
Provides information relevant to the curriculum used in the student's classes e.g., can interpret graphs and charts in the science text; however, much of the vocabulary is too difficult for the student to decode and understand. Cannot read or understand classroom text independently.	Unrelated to the student's curriculum: relies solely on norm-referenced data e.g., 6.2 grade equivalent in decoding skills
Specific: provides functional achievement levels and strengths and weaknesses in skill development. e.g., can read 3rd grade materials fluently and with 90% comprehension. Reads grade-level text (5th grade) very haltingly with many decoding errors and poor comprehension.	General e.g., Cannot read on grade level
Yields curriculum-based information that can be used to adjust instruction and monitor progress e.g., using a text reader when reading the science text; progress checked on chapter vocabulary tests, Tier 2 & 3 progress monitoring	Vague description (student is behind peers and is not meeting grade-level expectations)
Is tailored to the specific presenting needs of the student, practices vary depending on the student's needs e.g., can construct a paragraph on a computer	A standard battery that is collected on all students, regardless of the presenting needs/problems e.g., Istation scores at 40% cut score

Classroom Achievement

Is the student's achievement very different from others in his or her grade?

Analyzing data with regard to classroom achievement requires the RtI team to gather relevant and specific information about the student's performance in the general education curriculum in order to compare the student's achievement to same age and ability peers. In general, this means students in the same grade as the student being evaluated:

- ✓ determine if a pattern of student failure in classroom achievement in one or more areas has existed over time; and
- ✓ provide information about the instructional demands. This includes the curriculum, instructional context and strategies used with all students, as well as modifications used with the student being evaluated (ICEL).

When collected data do not present a clear and consistent story, there must be an examination of potential reasons for inconsistencies, including the validity of data and potential factors that might have led to variable performance across tasks or settings. The analysis of classroom achievement assumes that the student has received *adequate opportunities to learn and reasonable instructional options* within general education.

Does the student meet the educational standards that apply to all students?

The analysis of classroom achievement MUST provide instructionally relevant information about the student's performance in the general education curriculum.

(RtI Tier 1) Data on classroom achievement include:

- Description of instruction provided
- Description of learning environment
- District/classroom expectations and criteria for measuring progress/success
- Individual achievement data
- Student work samples/portfolios
- Formative assessment data (checklists, observations, quiz scores, teacher notes, etc.)
- Data about behavior, attendance, other factors
- Background information, historical data
- Comparative data of peer performance

Curriculum-Based Data

Curriculum-based information can easily be obtained during daily instruction and observation. This information allows for direct comparison with other age and grade classmates. Data collected as part of daily instruction can also be used to compare progress within the curriculum and describe achievement in instructionally relevant language. A summary of results from such data might include:
"When given materials used in her classroom, the student read very slowly. She had great difficulty blending sounds together. She had adequate comprehension of stories read to her and used picture clues to help her understand when prompted. She did not remember to use such clues when observed reading by herself. She seemed to get so bogged down trying to figure out the words, she forgot to use other reading strategies. Her reading level as measured by an informal reading inventory was primer."

Reminder: *One data source in isolation is never used for problem solving!*

Neither standard scores nor grade equivalents from individually administered diagnostic instruments can be used to determine whether a student has a severe delay in classroom achievement. These normative scores do not provide specific information about the student's actual performance when using classroom curriculum. Standard scores and grade equivalents do not indicate whether the student can read text used in his or her classroom or the degree to which the student is making progress toward achieving district standards.

There are several other sources of data that may not be used as the sole documentation for classroom achievement delay. Scores on statewide and district standardized tests and report card grades, while providing an indication of academic achievement, may also reflect other factors such as motivation, classroom behavior, and work completion.

Instructional Demands

What are the academic task requirements for students in the identified student's classroom?

Guiding question for gathering data: **What has been taught to the student and how?**

Staff must examine the student's ability to meet the instructional demands of the classroom. Instructional demands refer to the type and level of academic and behavioral performance teachers expect students to meet (e.g., "'all fourth-grade students are expected to independently read and comprehend material from trade books). When applying the classroom achievement criterion, the degree to which the identified student meets that specific task requirement must be compared to the performance of all of the students in his or her classroom.

Measured through observation:

- ✓ relate to the teacher's stated area of concern;
- ✓ identify instructional strategies, interventions, or accommodations that have been or are being used;
- ✓ describe how the student performs in the area(s) of suspected underachievement compared to other students;
- ✓ verify or add information to teacher perceptions of the presenting problem;
- ✓ cross-validate observations made by team member(s) or teachers in other settings;
- ✓ describe the student's functioning level in large and small group settings; and
- ✓ relate observed behavior to the student's academic functioning

Achievement

Is the student's achievement very different from others in his or her grade? *Does the student's achievement fall far outside the range of most other grade-level peers? Is the student's performance so different that the student cannot meet expectations even with sufficient general education instruction, intervention, and varied instructional approaches?*

Guiding questions for gathering achievement data include the following:

- Has the student received instruction on the same content as the majority of students in the same grade?
- What are the student's skills in relation to what has been taught?
- What is the range of student skill levels?
- Are there any other children performing at the same level as the identified student?

Sources of classroom achievement data:

- work samples
- error analysis
- criterion-referenced measures
- task analysis
- Curriculum-based measures: inventories, quizzes, rubrics, running records, informal reading inventories
- record review
- others that indicate classroom learning

Work Samples

Gathering work samples is relatively easy. Most teachers retain at least some student work. When teachers use portfolios there will be a wide range of work samples from which to choose. However, not all work samples are equally useful, so it is important to select samples in the areas of identified student concern and to collect them intentionally so that they adequately represent the areas that you are analyzing. It is highly recommended that the team review work samples that represent a student's work in the classroom over time.

Assessment: CBMs

Timely, reliable assessments indicate which students are falling behind in critical skills or which students need to accelerate their learning. Such assessments allow teachers to design instruction that responds to the students' learning needs. Progress monitoring (i.e., CBM) is conducted frequently and is designed to:

- Estimate rates of student improvement
- Identify students who are not demonstrating adequate progress
- Compare the efficacy of different forms of instruction and design more effective, individualized instructional programs for problem learners

What questions are we trying to answer with our student progress data?
- Is the student making progress in the classroom?
- Will the student pass the STAAR test?
- Should alternative instruction be used?
- Should an alternative placement be considered?
- Do the student data indicate a disability condition?

How to use universal screening data
Analyzing trends
Classroom instruction: Lesson planning, flexible grouping, differentiated instruction

Using data for progress monitoring
General Procedures
- Select goal-level material
- Collect baseline data and set realistic or ambitious goals
- Administer timed, alternate measures weekly
- Apply decision-making rules to graphed data every 3 or 4 weeks
- Implement instructional interventions when warranted
- Use database to analyze errors and to develop instructional procedures

Appendix E

RIOT/ICEL Matrix

An organizing framework for the comprehensive analysis of problem solving, referred to as RIOT/ICEL, is recommended by Hosp (2006). The data are organized within the table format shown here, in which the top horizontal row includes the sources of data collection (RIOT: review, interview, observe, test). The left column includes the domains of learning to be reviewed (ICEL: instruction, curriculum, environment, learner).

RIOT/ICEL data collection format

Domains of Learning	Sources of Data Collection			
	Review	Interview	Observe	Test
Instruction				
Curriculum				
Environment				
Learner				

Using this matrix as a guide, the team enters multiple data sources into the appropriate sections to aid in providing a comprehensive summary of the learner. The examples on the following pages demonstrate how data in these domains will help to explain the degree to which teacher-differentiated strategies and accommodations, curriculum demands/resources, environmental influences, and learner-specific variables affect the student's ability to demonstrate growth.

RIOT/ICEL: Framework for organizing data sources

	REVIEW	INTERVIEW	OBSERVE	TEST
INSTRUCTION	Describe the primary mode of instructional delivery and expected production. Pace and delivery of instruction. Is this consistent with student needs? Relevance	Academic engagement of student when instruction delivery is aligned to learning preferences and processing. What instructional strategies or accommodations work best for student? Generalization	What do classroom observations indicate? (e.g., differentiated techniques such as scaffolding are very helpful along with the use of graphic organizers. Lecture does not work well. Student shows latency in responding to first requests on writing tasks.)	What do formative assessments indicate about instructional level of content? Is it appropriate? Use baseline data from multiple sources. **Use progress monitors, diagnostic assessments, and criterion-referenced assessments.** **Appropriateness**
CURRICULUM	Textbook—grade level and instructional level skills addressed through permanent products, computer-aided instruction, and other curriculum resources. **How do you know?** Relevance	Core curriculum at grade level, additional resources added to supplement skill deficit area of disability. **What aspects of the disability/processing affect interaction with core curriculum?** Generalization	Exposure to core curriculum and added facilitated supports. **How, when, and is it enough?**	What is the instructional level and vocabulary level of the curriculum delivery? **Does it match baseline data from multiple sources? Align standards with data on student achievement.** **Are supports evidence based?** **Appropriateness**
ENVIRONMENT	General education setting. **Student-teacher ratio?** **Other student variable?** **Classroom management?** Relevance	Variables: e.g., does better with study buddy, use of visuals, proximity control for academic engagement. Small group instruction for grade-level reading. Generalization	Rules are easily observed, classroom noise, movement, immediate feedback and redirect observations. **Classroom organization is essential for the struggling student.**	Essential discipline data for individual student and classroom trends are used as a baseline for strong organizational and classroom variables as they relate to the environment. Heterogeneous grouping, instructional grouping, etc. **Are instructional groups designed and aligned with student data?** **Appropriateness**
LEARNER	Multiple data sources used to determine academic and behavioral strengths and weaknesses. Relevance	Describe student's learning strategies, capabilities, and weaknesses. Generalization	Student's engagement, production habits, and response to feedback, peer support, etc.	Use multiple data sources: universal screening, progress monitoring, formative, summative, diagnostic assessments. Review RTI, FIE, IEP. **Appropriateness**

RIOT/ICEL: Framework for organizing data sources (example, fourth-grade student)

	REVIEW	INTERVIEW	OBSERVE	TEST
INSTRUCTION	Primary mode of instruction is auditory (lecture) with independent learning activities (worksheets and group discussion). Note: Past report cards indicate he responds well to hands-on activities and does poorly when given worksheets.	Teacher(s) report academic engagement is enhanced when information is presented with visual cues, chunked into smaller segments, and paired with manipulatives.	Classroom observations indicate that differentiated techniques such as scaffolding are very helpful along with the added use of graphic organizers. Lecture does not work well.	Formative assessments are primarily worksheets with weekly computer-generated assessments from curriculum-supported computer-aided instruction.
CURRICULUM	Textbook– grade level, permanent products are a combination of worksheets, small group activities Tier 2: MVRC Reading Tier 3: F&P LLI kits	Math curriculum at grade level, reading added Tier 2 and 3 instruction Has been in Tier 2 instruction 18 weeks and Tier 3 2 weeks.	On MVRC for Tier 2 and LLI for Tier 3 added instruction. Instructional level is 2nd grade.	
ENVIRONMENT	Grade level 24 students, 1 teacher. Well organized classroom with structure in place for task engagement. PBIS: Character Ed program: Capturing Kids Hearts	Student does better with peer study buddy, use of visuals, proximity control for increasing engagement. Small group instruction for grade-level reading.	Rules are easily observed, classroom noise is moderate, lots of movement, immediate feedback and redirect observed Tier 2: computer lab Tier 3: Small group 3:1	
LEARNER	Grade-level math Below grade level in reading. There is history of failure on first classroom assessment attempt, passes on second, no sig. dev. History, referred to RtI for first time in 3rd grade. Tutorials in past have not been successful.	Teacher frustrated with lack of progress in reading comprehension, fluency has increased since using Read Naturally every morning as warm-up. Father had difficulty reading. No medical history noted.	Student is very quiet in class, does not volunteer to participate; he tends to let peers do all the work. Poor academic engagement: TOT: 70%, proximity control works well. Does not initiate questions. Responds to positive praise.	US: 24th percentile based on cutoff score (ISIP) PM: ROI .52 on 2nd grade PM: Reading 43 WCPM. Did not meet six week goal; Unit assessments: 63%, Failed STAAR Currently C average.

Reasons for intensifying intervention? Reading fluency and reading comprehension.
Areas targeted for intervention? Reading fluency, reading comprehension

Glossary

Abbreviations

BOY, MOY, EOY beginning, middle, and end of year

CBM curriculum-based measurement

ESEA Elementary and Secondary Education Act

ESSA Every Student Succeeds Act

IDEA Individuals with Disabilities Education Improvement Act of 2004

IEE independent educational evaluation

IEP individualized education plan

LLI Leveled Literacy Intervention

NASDSE National Association of State Directors of Special Education

NCLB No Child Left Behind Act

NRCLD National Research Center on Learning Disabilities

PD professional development

ROI rate of improvement

RtI Response to Intervention

WCPM words correct per minute

Terms

aimline A visual representation (line) on a progress monitoring graph that connects the baseline data point to the outcome goal.

align To reorganize and modify components as needed so that they form a unified system.

antecedent event An event that triggers a problem behavior.

assessment The process of using evaluation tools to gather and analyze information about student skill level and progress and the effectiveness of curricula and teaching methods.

baseline data point An initial score that indicates a student's skill level before intervention; serves as the starting point in curriculum-based measurement of the student's response to the intervention.

campus RtI team A campus-level team of teachers, counselors, administrators, and support personnel who meet on a regular basis to discuss data-based instructional solutions for students who are demonstrating difficulty progressing on grade-level content within the general education setting.

consequence What happens immediately after a behavior occurs.

criterion-referenced assessment A measure of performance in terms of a clearly defined learning task.

curricular variable A quantifiable event or circumstance related to the instruction of students in the schools.

curriculum The set of courses, coursework, and content offered at a school.

curriculum-based measurement (CBM) Any set of assessment procedures that use direct observation and recording of a student's performance in a local curriculum to gather information for making instructional decisions.

cutoff score Within RtI, a preset score set to help identify struggling learners during universal screening at Tier 1. The most common cutoff score used by school districts is set at the 25th percentile based on local, state, or national norms.

data-point decision rule A means of interpreting curriculum-based measurement data (points on a graph) in order to make decisions about a student's intervention plan.

decision points Guidelines developed by the district for gauging whether a student may need more intensive interventions within the RtI process.

delivery of instruction The methods for introducing information to students.

developmental skill progression The process of acquiring the basic skills necessary for learning to occur.

diagnostics A precise form of assessment that analyzes individual student strengths and weaknesses.

differentiated instruction An approach to teaching and learning in which students have multiple options for taking in information and making sense of ideas; requires teachers to be flexible in adjusting their methods and the curriculum to suit students, rather than expecting students to modify themselves for the curriculum.

direct observations Systematic, structured observations that use well-designed observation record forms.

documentation Any material (such as student products, tests, written reports) containing data gathered during the RtI process.

educational diagnostician A professional with an ability to assess and diagnose the learning problems of students.

eligibility conditions Conditions defined by federal and state governments for determining whether children qualify to receive special education services.

emotional disturbance eligibility Qualification of a student as eligible to receive special supports to counteract a chronic behavior or emotional condition that adversely affects his or her educational performance.

environmental triggers Events or situations in the student's environment that bring about a behavioral response.

fidelity The degree to which something is carried out as designed, intended, or planned.

fluency An acceptable level of mastery of a skill.

focused student-based interventions Interventions designed for individual students that are focused on specific foundational skills necessary for student learning.

foundational skills A set of skills students must master before they can become fluent in reading or math.

full and individual evaluation A comprehensive set of data gathered from multiple sources for each student being considered for special education and related services.

functional behavioral assessment A collection of information about events that predict and maintain a student's problem behavior; used to construct a behavior action plan.

functional communication The use of language in a meaningful and understandable way.

hypothesis statement In the functional behavioral assessment, the statement that identifies the function that maintains a student's problem behavior (what the student gets out of the behavior).

IEP team The group of people responsible for developing, reviewing, and revising an individualized education plan.

independent educational evaluation (IEE) As defined by IDEA, "an evaluation conducted by a qualified examiner who is not employed by the public agency responsible for the education of the child in question" (34 CFR 300.502).

individualized education plan (IEP) Either the educational program to be provided to a child with a disability or the written document that describes that program. Public schools are required by IDEA to develop an IEP for every student with a disability who meets the federal and state requirements for special education.

instruction The act of delivering information so that learning can occur.

instructional effectiveness A measure of a teacher's delivery of instruction, based on the positive learning outcomes of students.

instructional variable A quantifiable event or circumstance related to the action, practice, or profession of teaching.

intervention Any process that has the effect of increasing learning or modifying a student's behavior.

interventionists Persons trained in specific aspects of academic and behavioral interventions.

intrinsic motivation Motivation that is governed by an individual's internal drives.

learning difference A difference between the student's performance and that of typical peers or expected standards.

learning disability As defined by IDEA, "a disorder in one or more of the basic psychological processes involved in understanding or in using language, spoken or written, that may manifest itself in an imperfect ability to listen, think, speak, read, write, spell, or do mathematical calculations, including conditions such as perceptual disabilities, brain injury, minimal brain dysfunction, dyslexia, and developmental aphasia." Learning disabilities do *not* include "learning problems that are primarily the result of visual, hearing, or motor disabilities, of mental retardation, of emotional disturbance, or of environmental, cultural, or economic disadvantage" (34 CFR 300.8).

learning rate The pace of a student's skill acquisition; one of the elements used for making decisions in RtI.

learning style The method of learning, individualized to a student, that allows the student to learn most easily and effectively.

norm-referenced assessment A measure of performance in terms of an individual's standing in some known group, such as all of a district's students at a particular grade level.

operational definition A description of behaviors that are observable and measurable.

outcome goal The targeted goal of an intervention plan.

paraeducators Support members of the learning and teaching team who ensure that students receive multiple levels of support in schools.

passive noncompliance The failure of a student to perform a teacher's request, often by acting as if he or she did not hear it.

peer-assisted learning A specific research-based intervention that uses class-wide peer tutoring techniques developed by Doug and Lynn Fuchs.

performance Measurable outcomes that are characteristic of student learning.

performance deficit An inability to demonstrate a skill that has been learned.

phoneme segmentation The ability to break up and identify the sounds within words.

phonemic awareness Awareness of the sounds of language and how they make up words and sentences.

phonics An instructional design that involves teaching children to read by connecting sounds with letters or groups of letters.

positive behavior support system A systematic approach that clearly establishes behavioral expectations and uses reinforcement when the student demonstrates appropriate behaviors.

positive reinforcement The process of associating a desired behavior with a desired consequence, which then increases the probability that the behavior will be repeated.

pre-referral assessment An evaluation of whether further assessment is needed to determine a student's special education eligibility. This type of assessment does not focus on developing intervention strategies.

preventive Refers to action (such as early intervention) undertaken to avoid failure.

proactive Refers to action that anticipates future needs or problems, such as putting supports in place to increase the probability of successful learning outcomes and positive behaviors in the classroom.

probes In terms of progress monitoring and curriculum-based measurement, refers to brief repeated assessments of an academic skill.

problem behavior Behavior that has been identified as impeding the learning of the student or of others in the student's environment.

problem-solving method A set of specific steps for solving problems related to the challenging aspects of teaching and learning.

professional learning community A group of teachers in a grade-level or content area who meet regularly and work collaboratively to improve their teaching skills and the academic performance of students.

progress monitoring Frequent measurement of student progress in a brief, repeatable, reliable, and scientifically valid way; usually performed at predetermined intervals to allow for timely modification of instructional design to suit the student's needs.

prosocial behaviors Actions that are intended to benefit others in social situations.

Reading First initiative A process whereby states and districts receive support from the federal government for applying scientifically based research to ensure that all children learn to read well by the end of third grade.

referral-to-test model A service delivery model in which a student must be referred to a campus team and tested for eligibility before receiving special education supports and services.

research-based strategies Instructional designs and recommendations that have been demonstrated through formal scientific research to improve learning.

retention rate A measure of a student's ability to retain and demonstrate a previously learned skill.

RtI model A conception of the process known as Response to Intervention for delivering scientifically based instruction and interventions to facilitate student learning.

screening A type of assessment used to predict which students are likely to experience difficulty learning.

Section 504 Part of the federal Rehabilitation Act of 1973 that protects individuals with disabilities against discrimination. The civil rights of students in school settings are protected under Section 504, which requires a school district to provide a "free appropriate public education" (FAPE) to each qualified student with a disability who is in the school district's jurisdiction, regardless of the nature or severity of the disability. Regular or special education and related aids and services must be designed to meet the student's individual educational needs as adequately as the needs of nondisabled students are met.

Section 504 committee A school-based team that meets to discuss the needs of a student with a disability condition and how the condition affects learning. (Section 504 is a federal law that prohibits discrimination against individuals with disabilities.)

service delivery model A description of the way in which services—such as classroom placement, strategic interventions, peer tutoring, cooperative grouping, and differentiated instruction—will be provided to students.

setting event An event that is removed in time from the occurrence of a problem behavior but is related to it.

SIOP model Sheltered Instruction Observation Protocol: An excellent resource for supporting the educational needs of culturally and linguistically diverse student populations.

skill deficit A deficiency in a skill that is necessary for learning to occur or for achieving competence in a given area.

sound blending The blending of sounds together to form words.

staff development Intensive and ongoing training for teachers, administrators, and educational specialists, with a goal of improving the performance of both staff and students.

standardized assessment A type of test that is developed according to standard procedures and is administered and scored in a consistent manner for all students.

standard protocol Interventions that match a set of research-based practices to students who show predictable patterns of performance.

structural variables Quantifiable events or circumstances related to a school system's pattern of organization.

structured observation technique A formal method of observing students within the school environment.

struggling learners Students with characteristics that indicate they have a higher chance of failing in the areas of learning and behavior.

student product Something created by a student to demonstrate learning of a skill.

student-based interventions Interventions specifically designed for individual students.

sustainable problem-solving process A set of principles and procedures that guide instruction and intervention in ways that can be maintained and defended over time.

tiers of intervention Levels of increasingly intense interventions to help students learn.

universal strategies Instructional and behavioral strategies that are available to all students.

validity The degree to which a test measures what it was designed to measure.

within-student issue An issue that is due to a student's learning and emotional/behavioral strengths and weaknesses.

Bibliography

Batsche, G., J. Elliott, J. L. Graden, J. Grimes, J. F. Kovaleski, D. Prasse, D. J. Reschly, J. Schrag, and W. D. Tilly III. 2005. *Response to Intervention: Policy considerations and implementation*. Alexandria, VA: National Association of State Directors of Special Education.

Cheramie, G., and A. Ogonosky. 2016. Training materials designed for professional guidance and use, distributed by the authors. Houston: Ogonosky Learning.

Deno, S. L. 1987. Curriculum-based measurement: An introduction. *Teaching Exceptional Children* 20: 41–44.

Deno, S. L., A. Reschly-Anderson, E. Lembke, H. Zorka, and S. Callender. 2002. A model for schoolwide implementation: A case example. Paper presented at the National Association of School Psychologists, Chicago.

Echevarria, J., C. Richards-Tutor, and M. E. Vogt. 2015. *Response to Intervention (RTI) and English learners: Using the SIOP model*. 2nd ed. Manufactured in the United States of America: Pearson Education.

Englemann, S., and D. Carmine. 1982. *A theory of instruction, principles, and applications*. New York: Irvington.

Every Student Succeeds Act of 2015 (ESSA). PL 114–95. www.govtrack.us/congress/bills/114/s1177.

Fisher, D., N. Frey, and J. Hattie. 2016. *Visible Learning for literacy: Implementing the practices that work best to accelerate student learning*. Thousand Oaks, CA: Corwin Literacy.

Fountas, I., and G. Pinnell. 2016. *Guided reading: Responsive teaching across the grades*. Portsmouth, NH: Heinemann.

Fountas, I., and G. S. Pinnell. *Leveled Literacy Intervention System*. fountasandpinnell.com/lli. Portsmouth, NH: Heinemann.

Fuchs, D., and L. S. Fuchs. 2005. Responsiveness-to-intervention: A blueprint for practitioners, policymakers, and parents. *Teaching Exceptional Children* 38(1): 57–61.

Fuchs, D., L. Fuchs, J. Hintz, and E. Lenke. 2006. Progress monitoring in the context of Responsiveness to Intervention. Paper presented at the National Center on Student Progress Monitoring Summer Institute, Kansas City, MO.

Fuchs, L. S., C. L. Hamlett, and D. Fuchs. 1999. *MBSP: Monitoring Basic Skills Progress*. Austin, TX: Pro-Ed.

Good, R. H., J. Gruba, and R. A. Kaminski. 2001. Best practices in using

Dynamic Indicators of Basic Early Literacy Skills (DIBELS) in an outcomes-driven model. In A. Thomas and J. Grimes, eds., *Best practices in school psychology* IV, 697–700. Washington, DC: National Association of School Psychologists.

Gordon, C. 2002. *Methods for measuring the influence of concept mapping on student information literacy.* Chicago: American Library Association.

Hargrove, L. J., and J. A. Poteet. 1984. Assessment in special education: The education evaluation. Englewood Cliffs, NJ: Prentice Hall.

Hasbrouck, J., and G. Tindal. 2017. *An update to compiled ORF norms* (Technical Report 1702). Eugene, OR: Behavioral Research and Teaching, University of Oregon.

Hattie, J. 2009. *Visible Learning: A synthesis of over 800 meta-analyses relating to achievement.* London and New York: Routledge.

Hattie, J., D. Fisher, and N. Frey. 2017. *Visible Learning for mathematics: What works best to optimize student learning.* Thousand Oaks, CA: Corwin.

Hosp, J. L. 2006 (May). Implementing RTI: Assessment practices and Response to Intervention. *NASP Communiqué* 34(7). Retrieved September 8, 2010, from http://www.nasponline.org/publications/cq/cq347rti.aspx

Individuals with Disabilities Education Improvement Act of 2004 (IDEA). PL 108-446. http://www.copyright.gov/legislation/pl108-446.pdf.

Jenson, W. R., H. K. Reavis, and G. Rhode. 1998. *The tough kid book.* Longmont, CO: Sopris West.

Jimerson, S. R., M. K. Burns, and A. M. VanDerHeyden. 2007. *Handbook of Response to Intervention: The science and practice of assessment and intervention.* New York: Springer.

Johnson, E., D. F. Mellard, D. Fuchs, and M. A. McKnight. 2006. *Responsiveness to Intervention (RtI): How to do it.* Lawrence, KS: National Research Center on Learning Disabilities.

Joseph, L. M. 2006. Incremental rehearsal: A flashcard drill technique for increasing retention of reading words. *Reading Teacher* 59: 803–807

Kaminski, R., and R. Good. 1998. Assessing early literacy skills in a problem solving model: Dynamic Indicators of Basic Early Literacy Skills. In M. R. Shinn, ed., *Advanced applications of curriculum-based measurement.* New York: Guilford.

Kilpatrick, J., J. Swafford, and B. Findell, eds. 2001. *Adding it up: Helping children learn mathematics,* published by Mathematics Learning Study Committee, National Research Council. Washington, DC: National Academy Press.

Knoff, H. M., and G. M. Batsche. 1995. Project ACHIEVE: Analyzing a school reform process for at-risk and underachieving students. *School Psychology Review* 24:579–603.

Kovaleski, J. F., E. E. Gickling, and H. Morrow. 1999. High versus low

implementation of instructional support teams: A case for maintaining
program fidelity. *Remedial and Special Education* 20:170–183.

Maxwell, J. C. 2000. *Failing forward: Turning mistakes into stepping stones for success.*
Nashville, TN: Thomas Nelson.

McCook, John E. 2006. *The RtI guide: Developing and implementing a model in
your schools.* Horsham, PA: LRP Publications.

McEwan-Adkins, E. K. 2010. *Forty reading intervention strategies for K-6 students:
Research-based support for RTI.* Bloomington, IN: Solution Tree Press.

McKenzie, Jamie. 2003. Inspired Investigations. *Educational Technology Journal*
12(5): 2003.

Méndez-Morse, S. 1992. *Leadership characteristics that facilitate school change.* Austin,
TX: Southwest Regional Development Laboratory.

NASDSE. 2005. *Response to Intervention: Policy considerations and implementation.*
Alexandria, VA: National Association of State Directors of Special Education.

National Joint Committee on Learning Disabilities. 2005. *Responsiveness to
intervention and learning disabilities.* http://www.ncld.org/index.php?
option=content&task=view&id=591.

National Staff Development Council. 2001. *Standards for staff development.* Rev.
ed. Oxford, OH.

No Child Left Behind Act of 2001 (NCLB). PL 107-110. http://www.ed.gov/
policy/elsec/leg/esea02/107-110.pdf.

Ownby, R., F. Wallbrown, A. D'Atri, and B. Armstrong. 1985. Patterns of
referrals for school psychological services: Replication of the referral
problems category system. *Special Services in the School* 1(4): 53–66.

President's Commission on Excellence in Special Education. 2002. *A new era:
Revitalizing special education for children and their families.* Washington, DC: U.S.
Department of Education.

Reid, M. I., L. R. Clunies-Ross, B. Goacher, and C. Vile. 1981. Mixed ability
teaching: Problems and possibilities. *Educational Research* 24(1): 3–10.

Sammons, L. 2016. *Implementing guided math: Tools for educational leaders.*
Huntington Beach, CA: Shell Education.

Sattler, J. M. 2002. *Assessment of children: Behavioral and clinical applications.* 4th ed.
La Mesa, CA: Jerome M. Sattler.

Schniedewind, N., and E. Davidson. 2000. Differentiating cooperative learning.
Educational Leadership 58(1): 24–27.

Shapiro, E. S. 1996. *Academic skills problems: Direct assessment and intervention.*
New York: Guilford.

Shinn, M. 1989. *Curriculum-based measurement: Assessing special children.* New
York: Guilford.

Showers, B., B. Joyce, and B. Bennett. 1987. Synthesis of research on staff
development: A framework for future study and state of the art analysis.
Educational Leadership 45(3): 77–87.

Sprick, R. 1998. *CHAMPs: A proactive and positive approach to classroom management.* Longmont, CO: Sopris West.

Tindal, G., J. Hasbrouck, and C. Jones. 2005. *Oral reading fluency: 90 years of measurement.* Eugene, OR: Behavioral Research and Teaching.

Tomlinson, C. A. 1995. Differentiating instruction for advanced learners in the mixed-ability middle school classroom. *ERIC Digest* E536 (October). http://www.ericdigests.org/1996-3/mixed.htm.

Wright, J. 2006. *CBM workshop manual.* http://www.interventioncentral.org.

 Dr. Andrea Ogonosky is a licensed psychologist, a licensed specialist in school psychology, and a nationally certified school psychologist who currently serves various roles in school districts across the United States. Her job duties include assessing students for IDEA disability conditions; conducting program reviews on Response to Intervention, Section 504, and Special Education; designing Response to Intervention systems of support for small, medium, and large school districts; providing professional development on a variety of educational and assessment topics; supplying expert testimony at local, state, and federal court; and supervising school psychology students at the master and doctoral level. Dr. Ogonosky has written five books on Response to Intervention and is a contributing author to *Woodcock-Johnson IV: Reports, Recommendations, and Strategies.* She began her educational career in Pennsylvania, where she was actively involved with the initial implementation of the Instructional Support Team process in that state. Since relocating to Houston, Texas, she has served in many capacities in school districts, from campus to central office leadership positions. Dr. Ogonosky served as an educational consultant with the Region 4 Educational Service Center prior to her current practice. She holds a doctorate in school psychology from the Pennsylvania State University and is a past president of the Texas Association of School Psychologists. Please contact Dr. Ogonosky at aogonosky@msn.com for additional information on RtI.